ADD ONE STITCH
KNITTING

Published in 2018 by Search Press Ltd.
Wellwood, North Farm Road,
Tunbridge Wells, Kent TN2 3DR

ISBN: 978-1-78221-570-7

QUMAOSK

This book was conceived, designed and produced by:
Quantum Books Ltd, an imprint of The Quarto Group
6 Blundell Street
London N7 9BH
United Kingdom

Publisher: Kerry Enzor
Editorial: Charlotte Frost, Julia Shone
Evaluator: Jodi Lewanda
Technical Consultant: Claire Creffield
Designer: Rosamund Saunders
Photographer: Simon Pask
Production Manager: Rohana Yusof

Printed in China by C&C Offset Printing Co., Ltd.

9 8 7 6 5 4 3 2 1

ADD ONE STITCH
KNITTING

Build up your skills stitch by stitch in
15 stylish projects

Alina Schneider

Search Press

CONTENTS

THE LESSONS

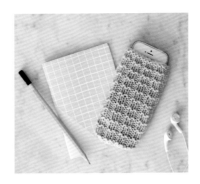

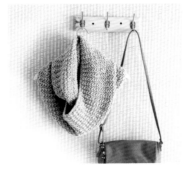

INTRODUCTION

The first time I picked up a pair of knitting needles and made a simple square in stocking stitch, I was thrilled! The idea that I could create something with a few simple tools fascinated me. At that point, I didn't know about the endless stitch combinations that can make such different textures, or how thrilling it is to discover new stitch patterns.

In this book, I hope to share my passion for knitting with you and introduce you to the stitches that you can use to create beautiful and simple handmade projects for your wardrobe and home. Each skein of yarn has great potential once you learn how to use it.

For me, each new design starts with the stitch. I have always been drawn to textures and I'm fascinated by how much depth and richness they give to the fabric. The diversity of stitch patterns makes me feel like a sculptor of fabric, as I can drastically change the look and feel of a design by choosing the right stitch combination.

It all starts with just two stitches – knit and purl. The beautiful thing about knitting is that even the most complex knitting patterns are repetitive and based on combining these two principal stitches. This book will walk you through the basics and give you the 'building blocks' that you will use for more complex projects in your future knitting journey. After following the lessons and making the projects from this book, you will realise that all knitted textures are created using different combinations of these two basic stitches, resulting in unique patterns.

I hope that this book will help you to fall in love with knitting and encourage you to explore the diverse range of stitch combinations, expand your knowledge and improve your skills with each new project.

Alina

TECHNIQUES

The following section will take you through all of the basic techniques you need to start knitting. Beginning with making a slip knot and casting-on, the chapter contains detailed instructions for using circular needles, as well as explaining how to knit and purl – the backbones of all knitting stitches! The chapter ends with guidance on giving your projects a neat and tidy finish.

GETTING STARTED

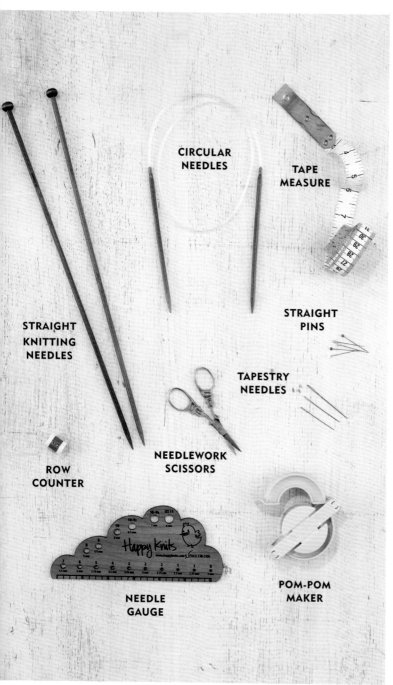

CIRCULAR
NEEDLES

TAPE
MEASURE

STRAIGHT
KNITTING
NEEDLES

STRAIGHT
PINS

TAPESTRY
NEEDLES

NEEDLEWORK
SCISSORS

ROW
COUNTER

NEEDLE
GAUGE

POM-POM
MAKER

Knitting Tools

Straight knitting needles come in a variety of materials including bamboo, aluminium and plastic. The type that you choose is down to personal preference; however, your needles should be smooth, with a nicely tapered tip, and preferably be lightweight to avoid straining your wrists.

Circular needles are two straight needles connected by a cord. It is important to choose the needles with the length of the cord slightly shorter than the circumference of the piece you are working on, otherwise the stitches will not stretch enough to be able to join the circle.

Tape measure Instead of repeating rows, it is common for patterns to instruct you to knit to a particular length before moving onto the next direction. A tape measure will help you keep track of the project dimensions.

Straight pins You will use pins when blocking your knitted items and aligning pieces for seaming.

Row counter helps you keep track of the number of rows worked.

Tapestry needles are used for seaming, weaving in ends and grafting stitches.

Needle gauge Even the same size needles can be of slightly different diameter, depending on the manufacturer, so it's helpful to be able to check the needle size.

Choosing and substituting yarn

Before you start any project, you should always take a look at the list of materials. Usually a knitting pattern will recommend a specific yarn that you should use to make the project, but if you can't get the suggested yarn or would like to use something else, you can always substitute.

When choosing yarn, keep these important points in mind:

Fibre content. Yarn can be made from a variety of fibres: animal, plant or synthetic materials. It is advisable to use the same type of fibre when changing yarns, as different fibres have varying properties that will create different results.

Yarn weight. Yarn weight indicates how thick the thread is, and is usually indicated on the yarn ball band. As yarn weight is a very important factor in achieving the recommended tension, it would make sense to substitute the recommended yarn with yarn of the same weight category.

Yardage. Before starting a project, you should know how much yarn to buy. If you are using the yarn specified in the pattern, simply buy the recommended number of balls. However, when substituting yarn, you need to consider the number of recommended balls as well as how much length is in these balls. For example, if the pattern recommends two balls of 91m (100yd) each and your substitute yarn comes in balls of 182m (200yd), you would need just one.

CATEGORIES OF YARN

Yarn	Lace including Fingering, 2ply and 10-count crochet thread	Super Fine including Fingering, Sock and Baby	Fine including Sport, 4ply and Baby	Light including DK and Light Worsted	Medium including Worsted, Aran and Afghan	Bulky including Chunky, Craft and Rug	Super Bulky including Super Chunky and Roving	Jumbo including Jumbo and Roving
Knit tension range in stockinng stitch to 10cm (4in)	33–40 sts	27–32 sts	23–26 sts	21–24 sts	16–20 sts	12–15 sts	7–11 sts	6 sts and fewer
Recommended needle in metric size range	1.5–2.25mm	2.25–3.25mm	3.25–3.75mm	3.75–4.5mm	4.5–5.5mm	5.5–8mm	8–12.75mm	12.75mm and larger
Recommended needle in US size range	000–1	1–3	3–5	5–7	7–9	9–11	11–17	17 and larger

How to check your tension

Tension refers to the number of stitches and rows per centimetre of your project. Usually the pattern gives you the number of stitches and rows or rounds (depending on whether you are knitting a piece flat or in the round) per 10cm (4in). Before starting any project, it is important to knit a swatch to check your tension. Even if you are using the same materials as stated in the pattern, it is still possible for your tension to be different from that stated in the pattern, meaning that your finished piece may not be the desired size.

TO CHECK YOUR TENSION:

Step 1 Check the tension listed in the pattern. Using the recommended size needles and specified yarn, cast on 10–20 stitches more than recommended for 10cm (4in). This will create a bigger swatch. The bigger the swatch, the more accurate your tension measurements will be. So, if the pattern recommends 16 stitches per 10cm (4in), cast on at least 26–30 stitches to create a bigger swatch.

Step 2 Work in the stitch pattern that you are going to use for your project for 12.5–15cm (5–6in) and then block it and allow it to dry.

Step 3 Use a tension measuring tool or tape measure to count the number of stitches and rows there are in 10cm (4in).

Step 4 If you have the same number of stitches and rows/rounds in 10cm (4in) as listed in the pattern, you can continue and begin knitting your project. If you have more stitches than recommended, it means that your tension is too tight and you should go up a needle size and make another tension square. If you have fewer stitches than expected, your tension is too loose and you should go down a needle size and make another tension square. You may need to make several swatches with different needle sizes to reach the correct tension.

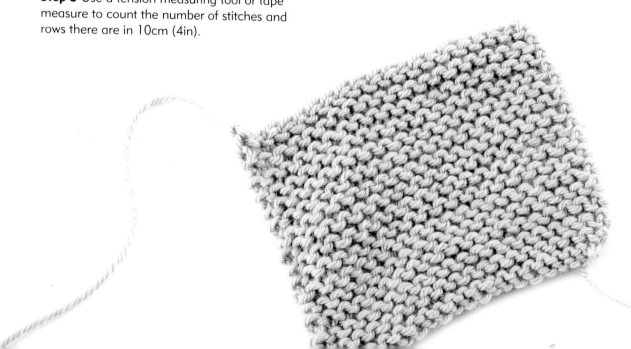

How to read a pattern in multiple sizes

Patterns for accessories and interior items usually give you one size option so that you just follow the instructions step by step. But when it comes to garments, it is important to understand how to read the pattern specifically for your size, otherwise you may read the wrong instructions and end up with a piece that is too big or too small for you.

Step 1 The first thing you should do is choose the correct size. The pattern will give you the information of body size or the actual measurements of the chest. This information is usually given at the beginning of a pattern. There are three sizes in the following example: small, medium and large.

> **BODY SIZE:**
> S (M, L) – 76 (91.5, 106.5) cm / 30 (36, 42) in at bust

Step 2 Take your measurements at the bust and choose the size that is closest to your bust circumference. It doesn't have to be an exact number, as knitting fabric is very forgiving. For example, if your bust measurement is 89cm (35in) and the pattern has only 76 or 91.5cm (30 or 36in) sizes available, choose the size that is closest – in this case, it is 91.5cm (36in).

Step 3 It is also important to pay attention to the 'ease' that is included within the pattern. 'Ease' is the extra width that is built into the garment to allow you to move comfortably in a knitted piece. If the pattern indicates that the intended ease should be + 5cm (2in), then your knitted garment will be 5cm (2in) bigger than your actual bust measurement in order to fit the way it was designed.

Step 4 After you've chosen your size, pay attention to the order in which the sizes are written:

> S (M, L)

All the numbers for each size will be written in the same order throughout the pattern. For example, if the pattern says:

> Sizes: S (M, L). Cast on 81 (95, 109) sts.

This means that you should cast on 81 sts for size S, 95 sts for size M and 109 sts for size L.

Step 5 Before starting the project, copy your pattern and highlight all the instructions that correspond to your size. This will make following the pattern a lot easier.

NOTE ON ABBREVIATIONS
Knitting patterns regularly abbreviate instructions and stitches. You can find a list of the stitch abbreviations used in the patterns in this book on page 126.

Slip knot

A slip knot is easy to tie and makes the first stitch of a
knitting project when you are casting on.

1 Wrap the yarn clockwise
around your index and
middle fingers, crossing it
over the other end of the
yarn to create a loop, and
leave a tail.

2 Pull a small amount of the
yarn through the loop to
make a new loop. Insert a
finger through this new loop,
holding onto the yarn end.

3 Pull the strands to tighten
up the knot, leaving a long
tail. The length of the tail
should relate to the number
of stitches you need to cast
on. Try to allow 2.5cm (1in)
of tail for each stitch.

Long-tail cast-on

There are many different ways to cast on,
but for ease I will cover the long-tail
cast-on. This method is great because it
only involves one needle and creates a very
neat cast-on edge.

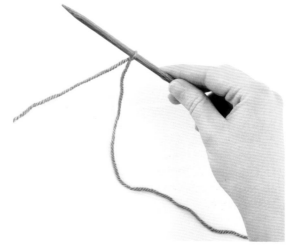

1 Place the slip knot onto a
needle and hold it in your
right hand.

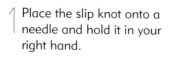

2 Insert your left thumb and index finger between the two strands of yarn, with the working yarn falling behind the index finger and the tail end of yarn in front of the thumb. Holding the two strands of yarn in your palm with your other fingers, spread your thumb and index finger apart to make a diamond shape with the yarn, with the tail end still over your thumb and the working yarn still over your index finger.

3 Insert the needle under the strand that is wrapped around your thumb.

4 Next, grab the strand that is wrapped around your index finger.

5 Pull a loop of yarn and the needle back through the thumb loop gently. Remove your thumb, leaving the new stitch on the knitting needle. Carefully pull the yarn to tighten the new stitch.

Repeat Steps 2–5 to cast on as many stitches as needed.

15

BASIC STITCHES

Knit stitch

The basis to all stitch patterns in knitting, knit stitch is the first stitch that you need to learn. Each stitch makes a 'bump' behind it, creating a raised row when it is worked continuously.

1 With the yarn at the back, insert the right needle knitwise into the next stitch on the left needle, from front to back, forming an 'x' with the right needle in the back.

2 Wrap the yarn around the right needle anticlockwise.

3 Draw the yarn through the stitch on the left needle to the front of the work. This will create a loop on the right needle.

4 Drop the original stitch off the tip of the left needle. You have made one new knit stitch on the right needle. Repeat Steps 1–4 to create more knit stitches.

Purl stitch

Fundamentally knit stitch in reverse, purl stitches create a great array of textural effects when they are paired with knit stitches in different combinations and arrangements.

1 With the yarn at the front, insert the right needle purlwise into the next stitch on the left needle, from back to front, forming an 'x' with the right needle at the front.

2 Wrap the yarn around the right needle anticlockwise.

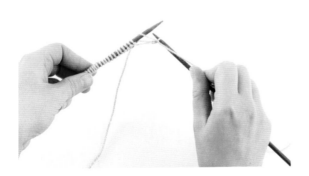

3 Draw the yarn through the stitch on the left needle to the back of the work. This will create a loop on the right needle.

4 Drop the original stitch off the tip of the left needle. You have made one new purl stitch on the right needle. Repeat Steps 1–4 to create more purl stitches.

The continental method

Whilst I prefer to use the English method of knitting (shown on pages 16-17), there is also another style known as the Continental method. The main difference here is that the yarn is held and controlled by the left hand rather than the right, as it is in the English method.

KNIT STITCH

1 Insert the right needle through the first stitch from left to right (front through to back) and lay the yarn across the tip.

2 Use the right needle tip to pull the next loop through, steadying the loop with your right index finger, if necessary. Allow the old stitch to drop from the left needle. Continue across the row in the same way or for as long as the pattern requires. When you reach the end, turn the work around to begin the next row.

PURL STITCH

1 Insert the right needle from right to left (back through to front) into the first stitch and lay the yarn anti-clockwise over the needle tip, pulling it downwards with your left index finger.

2 Use the right needle tip to carry the new loop back through the stitch, making a new stitch on the right needle and allowing the old stitch to drop from the left needle. Repeat as required.

Knitting in the round

Knitting in the round, or circular knitting, is a technique used to create a tube of fabric that doesn't need any assembly/seaming. Instead of working in rows back and forth, you work in rounds where the right side of the fabric is always facing you using circular needles.

1 Holding one end of the circular needle, cast on the stitches. Slide the stitches along the cord. The stitches must not be twisted and the cast-on edge should lie flat below the needle.

2 Insert the right needle into the first stitch on the left needle. It is important to knit this first stitch tightly to close the circle. Place a stitch marker onto the right needle after the final stitch.

3 Work the stitches as usual until you come to the stitch marker. This means that you have completed the first round. Slip the marker onto the right needle and work the next round.

Knitting flat with circular needles

Circular needles can also be used for knitting in rows. Straight needles are often not long enough to make big projects, but circular needles can fit a large number of stitches on the connecting cord. This makes them ideal for projects such as blankets and rugs.

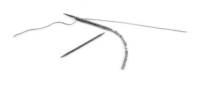

1 Cast on the required number of stitches.

2 Turn your work so that the end of the needle holding the stitches is in your left hand, and the other empty end is in your right.

3 Work across the stitches, following the instructions. Turn your work and continue throughout the pattern.

Magic loop

There is another method for knitting in the round – magic loop. It is mostly used to knit projects with a small circumference, using a circular needle.

1 Holding one end of the circular needle, cast on the required number of stitches. Turn the needle so the first cast-on stitch is on your left and the end with the working yarn is on your right.

2 Slide the stitches onto the cord and then divide them in two by pulling the cord between the centre stitches (it doesn't have to be an exact number; all you need is approximately the same number of stitches on each end of the cord).

3 Slide the stitches to the needle ends – the needle cord is now folded in half, dividing two sections of stitches. Pull the needle with the working yarn (on your right) so that all of its stitches slip off the needle and onto the cord.

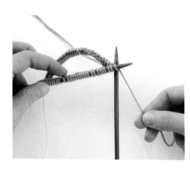

4 Holding the empty needle in your right hand and the needle containing half of the stitches in your left hand, start working across all the stitches on the left needle.

5 You have now worked half of the first round. The worked stitches are on the right needle with the working yarn; the left needle is now empty. Pull the cord so that the remaining (unworked) half of the stitches slide up onto the left needle. Pull the right needle so that the stitches just worked slide down onto the cord. Now work across the stitches on the left needle to complete the round. Continue working each round in this way.

Slipping stitches

Slip stitch is created by moving the stitch from the left needle to the right needle, without actually working it. It creates the decorative effect of an elongated stitch that stands out against the simple stitch background. Depending on the position of the working yarn and the way it is being slipped (either knitwise or purlwise), slip stitches create different visual results.

HOW TO WORK SLIP STITCH WITH YARN IN BACK

1 Bring the yarn between the needles to the back of the work.

2 Holding the working yarn in the back, insert the right needle into the next stitch purlwise and slide (or slip) the stitch from left needle to right needle, without working it.

HOW TO WORK SLIP STITCH WITH YARN IN FRONT

1 Bring the yarn between the needles to the front of the work.

2 Holding the working yarn in the front, insert the right needle into the next stitch purlwise and slide (or slip) the stitch from left needle to right needle, without working it.

Decreasing

Decreasing is a special technique that is used for both practical and decorative purposes. It is the process of removing stitches, making the fabric narrower. There are multiple ways of decreasing stitches, but the most common methods are knit two stitches together (k2tog) and purl two stitches together (p2tog).

K2TOG

3 Drop the stitches off the left needle (you have used two stitches to create one stitch, thus decreasing one stitch).

1 Insert the right needle knitwise into the next two stitches at the same time, from front to back.

2 Wrap the yarn around the right needle anticlockwise. Draw the yarn through the stitches on the left needle.

P2TOG

1 Insert the right needle purlwise into the next two stitches at the same time, from back to front.

2 Wrap the yarn around the right needle anticlockwise.

3 Draw the yarn through the stitches on the left needle. Drop the stitches off the left needle (you have used two stitches to create one stitch, thus decreasing one stitch).

FINISHING

Once your project is complete, there are a range of finishing and joining techniques that will make sure your designs are neat, tidy and long-lasting.

Casting off knitwise

1 Knit two stitches from the left needle. You now have two stitches on the right needle.

2 Insert the left needle from left to right into the front of the second stitch (counting from the needle tip); lift it over the first stitch and slip it off the needle. Knit the next stitch.

3 Repeat Step 2 across the row until all stitches are cast off in this way. When you have one stitch left, cut the yarn and pull the tail through the last stitch; tighten to secure the work.

Weaving in ends

1 Take your loose end and thread a tapestry needle onto the yarn.

2 Place the needle inside the first stitch along the bottom edge and push it through the stitch and the corresponding stitches several rows above.

3 Push the needle back down through the next column of stitches to the bottom edge. Repeat several more times until you feel that the yarn is secure.

Joining with Mattress Stitch

Probably the most used technique for joining knit pieces, mattress stitch creates an almost invisible, flexible and very neat vertical seam. It is also a very durable seam that at the same time has enough resilience not to pull on the fabric.

1 Lay the pieces to be seamed flat, with right sides facing up. Identify the horizontal threads running between the last stitch and the next-to-last stitch. You can find them by gently pulling the last two stitches apart. You will use these horizontal threads for the mattress stitch.

2 Thread a tapestry needle (try to use a blunt needle so that you don't split the stitches) and insert it into the bottom corner edge of the first piece from back to front. Pull the yarn through and insert the needle from front to back into the bottom corner edge of the opposite piece. You've now joined the two pieces together and can start the mattress stitch.

3 Find the horizontal thread between the first and the second stitches on the opposite knit piece. Insert the needle under the horizontal thread and pull the yarn through.

4 Insert the needle under the horizontal thread on the opposite piece and pull the yarn through.

5 Repeat Steps 3–4, working up the seam until you reach the top edge of the piece. You should have a seamless join.

Blocking

This is a finishing technique that is used to even out the stitches, open up lace and textured stitches, facilitate seaming and adjust the measurements of the knitted item if required. There is a big difference between unblocked and blocked knit fabric, so blocking should not be skipped. Different fibres will react differently to blocking. Be sure to always read the yarn label with the care instructions to avoid ruining your piece. The best way to check how your final piece will react to blocking is to first check it on your tension swatch or practice piece.

WET BLOCKING

Suitable for most types of fibre, although different fibres will take different amounts of time to dry. There are two ways you can use wet blocking.

1 First, place your knit piece in cool water; you can add a special soap for wool or even use a hair conditioner. Leave it in the water for 10–15 minutes, then gently squeeze out the water (do NOT twist or rub the fabric as it can cause felting). You can also wrap the piece in a towel and 'press' the excess water out.

2 Place the knit piece on a flat surface, stretch it to the measurements provided, and even out the stitches. You can pin the piece to a flat board to keep it in place. Allow it to dry completely.

3 You can also use a spray water bottle to wet block your knits. Pin the pieces to a flat board and spray with water. Allow it to dry completely.

STEAM BLOCKING

Not suitable for acrylic yarns or those that are handwash only (because these may felt with the heat from the iron). Generally speaking, if you are using cool water, spraying and don't press the fabric with the iron, it won't ruin your piece, except for novelty and lurex yarns – it is advisable to avoid blocking pieces knitted in those yarns.

1 Pin the item to a flat surface and, if needed, adjust to measurements. Use a basic steam iron or a steamer, held close to the fabric, but make sure NOT to touch the piece with the iron, otherwise it may ruin the knitted piece. Move the iron/steamer along the fabric until it is wet enough. Allow it to dry.

2 If preferred, you can cover your knit piece with a cloth before steam blocking.

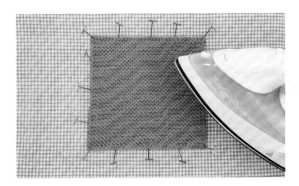

THE LESSONS

This section will introduce you to 15 stitch combinations that will create beautiful textures and patterns. From Stocking stitch and Rib, to Basketweave and Andalusian stitch, each lesson will take you through the basic principles and teach you to knit a tension swatch, before moving on to making stylish homewares or accessories.

LESSON | 1 # GARTER STITCH

Garter stitch is the easiest stitch pattern in knitting. It is created by simply knitting every single stitch on every row. This produces a dense and thick fabric that looks identical from both sides and lies perfectly flat; there is no curling or rolling of edges, which makes it perfect for simple accessories or interior pieces, such as scarves and blankets. Knitting every stitch on every row forms bumpy 'ridges' that run horizontally. As a result, garter stitch expands widthwise and is very elastic lengthwise, creating a stretchy but firm fabric. Knitting in garter stitch compresses the stitches slightly, so the fabric grows quite slowly and usually requires more yarn than the classic stocking stitch.

HOW TO KNIT GARTER STITCH

Garter stitch has a multiple of 1 stitch, so it is worked identically with both an even and odd number of stitches.

Row 1:

1 With the yarn at the back, insert the right needle knitwise into the next stitch on the left needle, from front to back, forming an 'x' with the needles.

2 Wrap the yarn around the right needle anticlockwise.

3 Draw the yarn through the stitch on the left needle to the front of the work to create a loop on the right needle. Drop the original stitch off the left needle (you have made one new knit stitch on the right needle).

Repeat Steps 1–3 until the end of the row.

PRACTICE PIECE

Yarn
Super chunky, 65% wool/35% alpaca, 100g (3½oz), 75m (82yd) in mid-grey.

Needles
9mm (US size 13)

Pattern
1 Using the long-tail cast-on method, cast on 16 sts.
Row 1 (RS): Knit.
Row 2 (WS): Knit.
2 Repeat Rows 1–2 until the piece measures approximately 12.5cm (5in) or the desired size.
3 Cast off knitwise. Weave in the ends.

GARTER STITCH SCARF

A simple garter stitch scarf is a classic knitting project. It is an ideal practice piece because garter stitch is solely made up of knit stitches, so it is very easy to make. The scarf doesn't really have to match the exact measurements, so any tension variations won't be that noticeable. Garter stitch creates a very dense and warm fabric that is perfect for a winter accessory. A long garter stitch scarf is a great 'zen' knitting project – just be sure to choose a yarn that you will really enjoy knitting with.

BEFORE YOU BEGIN

Techniques used
Casting on, see page 14
Slipping stitches, see page 21
Casting off knitwise, see page 23
Blocking, see page 25
Weaving in ends, see page 23

Project dimensions
Finished width: 33cm (13in);
finished length: 187cm (73½in)

Tension
9 sts measure 10cm (4in).
Row tension is not crucial for this project.

Yarn
4 balls of super chunky,
65% wool/35% alpaca,
100g (3½oz), 90m (98yd)
in dusky pink.

Equipment
9mm (US size 13) needles
Tapestry needle

PATTERN

1 Using the long-tail cast-on method, cast on 30 sts. The cast-on includes two selvedge stitches – one at the beginning and one at the end of each row, which are stitches that create a clean and tidy edge.

2 **Row 1 (RS):** Sl 1 st purlwise, knit to last st, knit the last st tbl.
Row 2 (WS): Sl 1 st purlwise, knit to last st, knit the last st tbl.

3 Repeat Rows 1–2 another 126 times or until the piece measures approximately 187cm (73½in) or the desired size.

4 Cast off knitwise.

Finishing

1 Block the piece.

2 Weave in the ends.

TIP

As garter stitch only has a one-row vertical repeat, you can easily modify the length of the scarf. Cast off as soon as you decide it's long enough.

STOCKING STITCH

Stocking stitch is one of the most basic and commonly used stitches in knitting. It is made up of the two main stitches, knit and purl, in their simplest combination. The right side of the project is formed by knit stitches; these create V-shaped columns that run vertically along the fabric, resulting in a smooth and even surface. The wrong side of the fabric is made of purl stitches; these produce little nubs that turn into horizontal ridges. The side edges are usually hidden within the seams; the bottom and top edges are usually trimmed with different variations of ribbing or any other stitch that lies flat, but in some cases the rolling of the fabric can be used as an interesting design element. Stocking stitch is very versatile – it is beautiful on its own, but can also serve as the perfect background for more complicated textured stitches.

HOW TO KNIT STOCKING STITCH

Stocking stitch has a multiple of 1 stitch, so it is worked identically with both an even and odd number of stitches.

RIGHT SIDE – KNIT STITCH
Row 1:

1 With the yarn at the back, insert the right needle knitwise into the next stitch on the left needle, from front to back, forming an 'x' with the needles.

2 Wrap the yarn around the right needle anticlockwise.

3 Draw the yarn through the stitch on the left needle to the front of the work to create a loop on the right needle. Drop the original stitch off the left needle (you have made one new knit stitch on the right needle).

Repeat Steps 1–3 until the end of the row.

WRONG SIDE – PURL STITCH
Row 2:

1 With the yarn at the front, insert the right needle purlwise into the next stitch on the left needle, from back to front, forming an 'x' with the right needle at the front.

2 Wrap the yarn around the right needle anticlockwise.

3 Draw the yarn through the stitch on the left needle to the back of the work to create a loop on the right needle. Drop the original stitch off the left needle (you have made one new purl stitch on the right needle).

Repeat Steps 1–3 until the end of the row.

TIP

To create a fabric with beautiful drape, try knitting stocking stitch in a lighter yarn with a larger than recommended needle size.

PRACTICE PIECE

Yarn
Super chunky, 100% wool, 100g (3½oz),
80m (87½yd) in cream.

Needles
9mm (US size 13)

Pattern
1 Using the long-tail cast-on method,
cast on 13 sts.
Row 1 (RS): Knit.
Row 2 (WS): Purl.
2 Repeat Rows 1–2 another six times.
3 Cast off knitwise. Weave in the ends.

FRONT: The right side of stocking stitch
is formed by knit stitches. These create
V-shaped columns running vertically
along the fabric.

BACK: The purl side of the fabric could also be
used as the 'right' side, in which case the stitch
pattern is called 'reverse stocking stitch'.

STOCKING STITCH CUSHION COVER

Add a touch of coziness to your living space with a simple cushion cover knitted in stocking stitch. Textiles are a cheap and easy way to decorate your home. Choose neutral and subdued colours for a minimalist and sophisticated look, or pick bright and cheerful shades to add colourful accents. Soft Peruvian highland wool knits up quickly and creates a wonderful stitch definition.

BEFORE YOU BEGIN

Techniques used
Casting on, see page 14
Knitting flat with circular needles, see page 20
Casting off knitwise, see page 23
Blocking, see page 25
Mattress stitch, see page 24
Invisible horizontal seam, see page 38
Weaving in ends, see page 23

Project dimensions
Finished width: 48.5cm (19in); finished height: 48.5cm (19in)

Tension
10 sts and 13 rows measure 10 x 10cm (4 x 4in). Row tension is not crucial for this project.

Yarn
3 balls of super chunky, 100% wool, 100g (3½oz), 80m (87½yd) in beige.

Equipment
9mm (US size 13) circular needle, 80cm (31in) long
Tapestry needle
Cushion insert, 51 x 51cm (20 x 20in) square

PATTERN

1 Using the long-tail cast-on method, cast on 47 sts.

Row 1 (RS): Knit.
Row 2 (WS): Purl.

2 Repeat Rows 1–2 until the piece measures 97cm (38 in) long.

3 Cast off knitwise.

Finishing

1 Block the piece.

2 Fold the cover in half the following way:
Wrong sides (purl sides) are together.
Cast-on and cast-off edges should be touching.

3 With right side facing, sew the right and left side edges together with mattress stitch.

4 Using a cushion insert that is 1.5–2.5cm (½–1in) larger than the cover, insert it into the opening on the knitted piece.

5 With right side facing, sew the cast-on and cast-off edges together with an invisible horizontal seam. Weave in the ends.

Invisible Horizontal Seam

A horizontal seam is ideal for joining two cast-off edges or one cast-on edge and one cast-off edge. This technique creates a neat and invisible seam that is perfect for joining shoulder seams or the parts of bags, for example.

1 Lay the pieces flat, with the right sides facing up, and the cast-off/cast-on edges facing each other. Line up the pieces stitch by stitch. (To create a neat seam, it is important to have the same number of stitches on each piece.)
2 Thread a tapestry needle with the same yarn you used for knitting the piece and insert the needle under a stitch inside the cast-off/cast-on edge on one side.
3 Insert the needle under a corresponding stitch inside the cast-off/cast-on edge on the other piece. Pull the yarn through.

Repeat Steps 2–3 until you have joined all the stitches.

TIP

To create a removable cover, sew buttons along one edge instead of seaming the cast-on and cast-off edges together.

1X1 RIB STITCH

1x1 rib stitch is one of the most popular types of ribbing; it is formed by alternating between one knit and one purl stitch. Because 1x1 rib is very elastic and stretchy, it is often used for trimming the hems of garments, sleeve cuffs and necklines, as well as for knitting accessories, such as hats, mitts and socks. When unstretched, 1x1 rib can look similar to columns of stocking stitch, with the purl stitches hidden between the knit columns; when stretched, the purl stitches will appear.

HOW TO KNIT 1X1 RIB STITCH

1x1 rib stitch has a multiple of 2 stitches. When knitting flat, to achieve a symmetrical look at each end, work the stitch pattern over an odd number of stitches.

RIGHT SIDE
Row 1:

1 With the yarn at the back, insert the right needle knitwise into the next stitch on the left needle, from front to back, forming an 'x' with the needles.

2 Wrap the yarn around the right needle anticlockwise.

3 Draw the yarn through the stitch on the left needle to the front of the work to create a loop on the right needle. Drop the original stitch off the left needle (you have made one new knit stitch on the right needle).

4 Bring the yarn between the needles to the front of the work.

5 With the yarn at the front, insert the right needle purlwise into the next stitch on the left needle, from back to front, forming an 'x' with the right needle at the front.

6 Wrap the yarn around the right needle anticlockwise.

7 Draw the yarn through the stitch on the left needle to the back of the work to create a loop on the right needle. Drop the original stitch off the left needle (you have made one new purl stitch on the right needle).

8 Bring the yarn between the needles to the back of the work.

Repeat Steps 1–8 until the last stitch of the row (alternate between one knit and one purl stitch).

9 With the yarn at the back, insert the right needle knitwise into the last stitch on the left needle, from front to back.

10 Wrap the yarn around the right needle anticlockwise.

11 Draw the yarn through the stitch on the left needle to the front of the work. Drop the original stitch off the left needle (this finishes the row with one knit stitch).

WRONG SIDE
Row 2:

1 With the yarn at the front, insert the right needle purlwise into the next stitch on the left needle, from back to front.

2 Wrap the yarn around the right needle anticlockwise.

3 Draw the yarn through the stitch on the left needle to the back of the work to create a loop on the right needle. Drop the original stitch off the left needle (you have made one new purl stitch on the right needle).

4 Bring the yarn between the needles to the back of the work.

5 With the yarn at the back, insert the right needle knitwise into the next stitch on the left needle, from front to back.

6 Wrap the yarn around the right needle anticlockwise.

7 Draw the yarn through the stitch on the left needle to the front of the work to create a loop on the right needle. Drop the original stitch off the left needle (you have made one new knit stitch on the right needle).

8 Bring the yarn between the needles to the front of the work.

Repeat Steps 1–8 until the last stitch of the row (alternate between one knit and one purl stitch).

9 With the yarn at the front, insert the right needle purlwise into the last stitch on the left needle, from back to front.

10 Wrap the yarn around the right needle anticlockwise.

11 Draw the yarn through the stitch on the left needle to the back of the work. Drop the original stitch off the left needle (this finishes the row with one purl stitch).

Repeat Rows 1–2 to form 1x1 rib stitch.

PRACTICE PIECE

Yarn
Chunky, 100% wool, 100g (3½oz), 117m (128yd) in purple.

Needles
5mm (US size 8)

Pattern
1 Using the long-tail cast-on method, cast on 19 sts.
Row 1 (RS): K1, *p1, k1; repeat from * across to end.
Row 2 (WS): P1, *k1, p1; repeat from * across to end.
2 Repeat Rows 1–2 until the piece measures approximately 12.5cm (5in).
3 Cast off knitwise. Weave in the ends.

1X1 RIB HAT

A classic knit hat is a true wardrobe staple. Stretchy 1x1 rib will create a snug fit and the folded brim will protect you from chilly winds. The hat is knit on a circular needle and doesn't require seaming. It is an easy, portable project that you can work on anywhere.

BEFORE YOU BEGIN

Techniques used
Casting on, see page 14
Knitting in the round, see page 18
Decreasing, see page 22
Weaving in ends, see page 23
Blocking, see page 25

Project dimensions
Finished circumference (when stretched): 56cm (22in); finished height (with hem unfolded): 30.5cm (12in)

Tension
14 sts and 22 rounds measure 10 x 10cm (4 x 4in) when stretched. Round tension is not crucial for this project.

Yarn
2 skeins of chunky, 100% wool, 100g (3½oz), 117m (128yd) in beige.

Equipment
5mm (US size 8) circular needle, 40.5cm (16in) long
Stitch marker
Tapestry needle

PATTERN

1 Using the long-tail cast-on method, cast on 78 sts. Join for working in the round, placing a stitch marker onto the right needle to mark the end of the round.

Rnd 1: *P1, k1; repeat from * to end of rnd.

2 Repeat Rnd 1 until the piece measures approximately 26.5cm (10½in).

3 Start the decrease rounds:

Dec Rnd 1: *K2tog; repeat from * to end of rnd – 39 sts left on the needles.

4 Knit 2 rnds.

5 **Dec Rnd 2:** *K2tog; repeat from * to last st of rnd, k1 – 20 sts left on the needles.

6 Knit 1 rnd.

7 **Dec Rnd 3:** *K2tog; repeat from * to end of rnd – 10 sts left on the needles.

8 Knit 1 rnd.

9 Cut the yarn, leaving a tail approximately 25.5cm (10in) long. Thread the tail through a tapestry needle and draw it through the remaining 10 sts, slipping them off the needle one by one. Pull tightly to gather the stitches together and 'close' the top of the hat. Insert a tapestry needle in the top of the hat and pull the yarn to the wrong side. Weave in the tail on the inside.

Finishing

1 Block the piece.

2 Weave in the ends.

2X2 RIB STITCH

2 x 2 rib stitch is made by alternating columns of two knit stitches and two purl stitches. It is one of many variations of ribbing and has many similarities to the classic 1x1 rib, creating reversible, textured and stretchy fabric, though it does have slightly less elasticity than 1x1 rib. It is used both as a stand-alone stitch and in combination with other stitch patterns, especially in garments. As the pattern repeat consists of only two rows, it is very easy to remember and relaxing to knit.

HOW TO KNIT 2X2 RIB STITCH

2 x 2 rib stitch has a multiple of 4 stitches. To achieve a symmetrical look at each end, add an extra 2 selvedge stitches to the end, so work the stitch pattern over a multiple of 4 stitches plus 2 additional stitches.

RIGHT SIDE
Row 1:

1 With the yarn at the back, insert the right needle knitwise into the next stitch on the left needle, from front to back, forming an 'x' with the needles.

2 Wrap the yarn around the right needle anticlockwise.

3 Draw the yarn through the stitch on the left needle to the front of the work to create a loop on the right needle. Drop the original stitch off the left needle (you have made one new knit stitch on the right needle).

4 Repeat Steps 1–3 once more (you have two knit stitches on the right needle).

5 Bring the yarn between the needles to the front of the work.

6 With the yarn at the front, insert the right needle purlwise into the next stitch, from back to front, forming an 'x' with the right needle at the front.

7 Wrap the yarn around the right needle anticlockwise.

8 Draw the yarn through the stitch on the left needle to the back of the work to create a loop on the right needle. Drop the original stitch off the left needle (you have made one new purl stitch on the right needle).

9 Repeat Steps 6–8 once more (you have two purl stitches on the right needle).

10 Bring the yarn between the needles to the back of the work.

Repeat Steps 1–10 until the last two stitches of the row (alternate between two knits and two purls).

Repeat Steps 1–4 (finishing the row with two knit stitches gives the work a symmetrical look).

WRONG SIDE
Row 2:

1 With the yarn at the front, insert the right needle purlwise into the next stitch on the left needle, from back to front.

2 Wrap the yarn around the right needle anticlockwise.

3 Draw the yarn through the stitch on the left needle to the back of the work to create a loop on the right

needle. Drop the original stitch off the left needle (you have made one new purl stitch on the right needle).

4 Repeat Steps 1–3 once more (you have two purl stitches on the right needle).

5 Bring the yarn between the needles to the back of the work.

6 Insert the right needle knitwise into the next stitch on the left needle, from front to back.

7 Wrap the yarn around the right needle anticlockwise.

8 Draw the yarn through the stitch on the left needle to the front of the work to create a loop on the right needle. Drop the original stitch off the left needle (you have made one new knit stitch on the right needle).

9 Repeat Steps 6–8 once more (you have two knit stitches on the right needle).

10 Bring the yarn between the needles to the front of the work.

Repeat Steps 1–10 until the last two stitches of the row (alternate between two purls and two knits).

Repeat Steps 1–4 (finishing the row with two purl stitches gives the work a symmetrical look).

Repeat Rows 1–2 to form 2 x 2 rib stitch.

PRACTICE PIECE

Yarn
Aran, 65% wool/35% alpaca, 50g (1¾oz), 75m (82yd) in pale blue.

Needles
4mm (US size 6)

Pattern
1 Using the long-tail cast-on method, cast on 26 sts.
Row 1 (RS): *K2, p2; repeat from * across to last 2 sts, k2.
Row 2 (WS): *P2, k2; repeat from * across to last 2 sts, p2.
2 Repeat Rows 1–2 until the piece measures approximately 12.5cm (5in).
3 Cast off in pattern (see page 50). Weave in the ends.

2X2 RIB STITCH LEG WARMERS

Bundle up your legs in a pair of cosy leg warmers. Easy to make and easy to wear, they make the perfect knitting project. The 2 x 2 rib pattern will ensure a snug fit, and a soft wool/alpaca blend will keep you comfy in any weather. Pair the leg warmers with boots for a great accessory.

BEFORE YOU BEGIN

Techniques used
Casting on, see page 14
Blocking, see page 25
Mattress stitch, see page 24
Weaving in ends, see page 23

Project dimensions
Finished circumference (when stretched): 40cm (15½in); finished length: 35.5cm (14in)

Tension
20 sts and 26 rows measure 10 x 10cm (4 x 4in) when slightly stretched. Row tension is not crucial for this project.

Yarn
4 balls of aran, 65% wool/35% alpaca, 50g (1¾oz), 75m (82yd) in light grey.

Equipment
4mm (US size 6) needles
Tapestry needle

PATTERN

Make two.

1 Using the long-tail cast-on method, cast on 78 sts.

Row 1 (RS): *K2, p2; repeat from * across to last 2 sts, k2.
Row 2 (WS): *P2, k2; repeat from * across to last 2 sts, p2.

2 Repeat Rows 1–2 until the piece measures 35.5cm (14in).

Cast off the stitches in pattern following the steps below.

3 K2 (you have two stitches on the right needle).

4 Insert the left needle from left to right into the front of the second stitch (counting from the needle tip); lift it over the first stitch and slip it off the needle. You have cast off one stitch (one stitch remains on the right needle).

5 Purl 1 stitch. Repeat Step 5.

6 Purl 1 stitch. Repeat Step 5.

7 Knit 1 stitch. Repeat Step 5.

8 Knit 1 stitch. Repeat Step 5.

9 Repeat Steps 6–9 across the row until one stitch remains on the right needle. Cut the yarn and pull the tail through the last stitch; tighten to secure the work.

Finishing

1 Block the piece.

2 Sew the side edges together with mattress stitch.

3 Weave in the ends.

SEED STITCH

Seed stitch is a 1x1 ribbing that is broken on every row, creating a textured fabric covered in little nubs that are arranged in chequerboard pattern. Seed stitch fabric doesn't roll or curl, but lies completely flat and looks identical on both sides, which makes it reversible and perfect for scarves, cowls, blankets or any other item where both sides can be seen. Knitted with smooth yarns, seed stitch looks sharp and crisp; fuzzy yarns, such as mohair, will give less stitch definition, but still give a very beautiful 'blurred' texture effect. Compared to classic ribbing, seed stitch takes more time to knit, as it has fewer stitches and more rows for every inch, but this creates a very firm and dense fabric, making it perfect for fall or winter garments and accessories.

HOW TO KNIT SEED STITCH

Seed stitch has a multiple of 2 stitches. When knitting flat, work the stitch pattern over an odd number of stitches to achieve a symmetrical look at each end. Note that if you choose to work over an even number of stitches, the instructions will be different; both methods are explained below.

RIGHT SIDE – ODD NUMBER OF STS

Row 1:

1 With the yarn at the back, insert the right needle knitwise into the next stitch on the left needle, from front to back, forming an 'x' with the needles.

2 Wrap the yarn around the right needle anticlockwise.

3 Draw the yarn through the stitch on the left needle to the front of the work to create a loop on the right needle. Drop the original stitch off the left needle (you have made one new knit stitch on the right needle).

4 Bring the yarn between the needles to the front of the work.

5 With the yarn at the front, insert the right needle purlwise into the next stitch on the left needle, from back to front, forming an 'x' with the right needle at the front.

6 Wrap the yarn around the right needle anticlockwise.

7 Draw the yarn through the stitch on the left needle to the back of the work to create a loop on the right

needle. Drop the original stitch off the left needle (you have made one new purl stitch on the right needle).

8 Bring the yarn between the needles to the back of the work.

Repeat Steps 1–8 until the last stitch of the row (alternate between one knit and one purl stitch).

9 With the yarn at the back, insert the right needle knitwise into the last stitch on the left needle, from front to back.

10 Wrap the yarn around the right needle anticlockwise.

11 Draw the yarn through the stitch on the left needle to the front of the work to create a loop on the right needle. Drop the original stitch off the left needle (this finishes the row with one knit stitch).

WRONG SIDE – ODD NUMBER OF STS

Row 2: Repeat Row 1.

RIGHT SIDE – EVEN NUMBER OF STS
Row 1:

1 With the yarn at the back, insert the right needle knitwise into the next stitch on the left needle, from front to back, forming an 'x' with the needles.

2 Wrap the yarn around the right needle anticlockwise.

3 Draw the yarn through the stitch on the left needle to the front of the work to create a loop on the right needle. Drop the original stitch off the left needle (you have made one new knit stitch on the right needle).

4 Bring the yarn between the needles to the front of the work.

5 With the yarn at the front, insert the right needle purlwise into the next stitch on the left needle, from back to front, forming an 'x' with the right needle at the front.

6 Wrap the yarn around the right needle anticlockwise.

7 Draw the yarn through the stitch on the left needle to the back of the work to create a loop on the right needle. Drop the original stitch off the left needle (you have made one new purl stitch on the right needle).

8 Bring the yarn between the needles to the back of the work.

Repeat Steps 1–8 until the end of the row (alternate between one knit and one purl stitch, and finish with the purl stitch).

WRONG SIDE – EVEN NUMBER OF STS
Row 2:

1 With the yarn at the front, insert the right needle purlwise into the next stitch on the left needle, from back to front.

2 Wrap the yarn around the right needle anticlockwise.

3 Draw the yarn through the stitch on the left needle to the back of the work to create a loop on the right needle. Drop the original stitch off the left needle (you have made one new purl stitch on the right needle).

4 Bring the yarn between the needles to the back of the work.

5 With the yarn at the back, insert the right needle knitwise into the next stitch on the left needle, from front to back.

6 Wrap the yarn around the right needle anticlockwise.

7 Draw the yarn through the stitch on the left needle to the front of the work to create a loop on the right needle. Drop the original stitch off the left needle (you have made one new knit stitch on the right needle).

8 Bring the yarn between the needles to the front of the work.

Repeat Steps 1–8 until the end of the row (alternate between one purl and one knit stitch, and finish with the knit stitch).

PRACTICE PIECE

Yarn

Aran, 55% wool/33% acrylic/12% cashmere, 50g (1¾oz), 90m (98yd) in beige.

Needles

4mm (US size 6)

Pattern

1 Using the long-tail cast-on method, cast on 21 sts.

Row 1 (RS): K1, *p1, k1; repeat from * across to end.

Row 2 (WS): Repeat Row 1.

2 Repeat Rows 1–2 another 19 times.

3 Cast off knitwise. Weave in the ends.

TIP

Always purl if you see a knit stitch, and always knit if you see a purl stitch.

SEED STITCH HEADBAND

A knitted headband is a great alternative to a hat when temperatures begin to warm up but you still need some cosy protection from cold winds. Wool blended with a touch of cashmere creates a great stitch definition that accentuates every 'nub' of the seed stitch. This is a very simple, straightforward project that is quick to make.

BEFORE YOU BEGIN

Techniques used

Casting on, see page 14

Slipping stitches, see page 21

Casting off knitwise, see page 23

Blocking, see page 25

Invisible horizontal seam, see page 38

Weaving in ends, see page 23

Project dimensions

Finished circumference: 47cm (18½in); finished width: 9.5cm (3¾in)

Tension

21 sts and 40 rows measure 10 x 10cm (4 x 4in). Row tension is not crucial for this project.

Yarn

1 ball of aran, 55% wool/33% acrylic/ 12% cashmere, 50g (1¾oz), 90m (98yd) in taupe.

Equipment

4mm (US size 6) needles

Tapestry needle

PATTERN

1 Using the long-tail cast-on method, cast on 21 sts. To create perfectly neat edges, the cast-on includes two selvedge stitches – one at the beginning and one at the end of each row.

Row 1 (RS): Sl 1 st purlwise, k1,*p1, k1; repeat from * across to last st, knit the last st tbl.
Row 2 (WS): Repeat Row 1.

2 Repeat Rows 1–2 until the piece measures approximately 47cm (18½in).

3 Cast off knitwise.

Finishing

1 Block the piece.

2 Sew the cast-on and cast-off edges together with an invisible horizontal seam.

3 Weave in the ends.

MOSS STITCH

Moss stitch is a slightly modified version of seed stitch. Instead of breaking up a 1x1 rib pattern every row as in seed stitch, for moss stitch you do it every other row. This small adjustment entirely changes the look of the fabric, creating elongated stitch columns running in diagonal order. As a result, moss stitch fabric is less firm and more stretchy. The fabric created by moss stitch is reversible and works great for any knit piece – from dishcloths to sweaters. It is also often used as a background for more complicated stitch patterns. Moss stitch is easily adapted for both flat and circular knitting. Items knitted in moss stitch do not require any special edge trim because the fabric lies flat and doesn't curl.

HOW TO KNIT MOSS STITCH

Moss stitch has a multiple of 2 stitches. When knitting flat, an extra stitch is added to the end to achieve a symmetrical look at each end. So work the stitch pattern over an odd number of stitches.

RIGHT SIDE
Row 1:

1 With the yarn at the back, insert the right needle knitwise into the next stitch on the left needle, from front to back, forming an 'x' with the needles.

2 Wrap the yarn around the right needle anticlockwise.

3 Draw the yarn through the stitch on the left needle to the front of the work to create a loop on the right needle. Drop the original stitch off the left needle (you have made one new knit stitch on the right needle).

4 Bring the yarn between the needles to the front of the work.

5 With the yarn at the front, insert the right needle purlwise into the next stitch, from back to front, forming an 'x' with the right needle at the front.

6 Wrap the yarn around the right needle anticlockwise.

7 Draw the yarn through the stitch on the left needle to the back of the work to create a loop on the right needle. Drop the original stitch off the left needle (you have made one new purl stitch on the right needle).

8 Bring the yarn between the needles to the back of the work.

Repeat Steps 1–8 until the last stitch of the row (alternate between one knit and one purl stitch).

9 With the yarn at the back, insert the right needle knitwise into the last stitch on the left needle, from front to back.

10 Wrap the yarn around the right needle anticlockwise.

11 Draw the yarn through the stitch on the left needle to the front of the work to create a loop on the right needle. Drop the original stitch off the left needle (this finishes the row with one knit stitch).

WRONG SIDE
Row 2:

1 With the yarn at the front, insert the right needle purlwise into the next stitch on the left needle, from back to front.

2 Wrap the yarn around the right needle anticlockwise.

3 Draw the yarn through the stitch on the left needle to the back of the work to create a loop on the right

needle. Drop the original stitch off the left needle (you have made one new purl stitch on the right needle).

4 Bring the yarn between the needles to the back of the work.

5 Insert the right needle knitwise into the next stitch on the left needle, from front to back.

6 Wrap the yarn around the right needle anticlockwise.

7 Draw the yarn through the stitch on the left needle to the front of the work. Drop the original stitch off the left needle (you have made one new knit stitch on the right needle).

8 Bring the yarn between the needles to the front of the work.

Repeat Steps 1–8 until the last stitch of the row (alternate between one purl and one knit stitch).

9 Insert the right needle purlwise into the last stitch on the left needle, from back to front.

10 Wrap the yarn around the right needle anticlockwise.

11 Draw the yarn through the stitch on the left needle to the back of the work. Drop the original stitch off the left needle (this finishes the row with one purl stitch).

RIGHT SIDE
Row 3: Repeat Row 2.

WRONG SIDE
Row 4: Repeat Row 1.

TIP

Changing needle size can drastically transform the look of your project. A tighter tension (using smaller needles) will result in a firm textured piece, whereas a looser tension (using larger needles) will produce a more openwork look.

Moss stitch captures light beautifully when knitted in light, neutral shades.

PRACTICE PIECE

Yarn
Chunky, 100% wool, 100g (3½oz),
117m (128yd) in fawn.

Needles
5.5m (US size 9)

Pattern
1 Using the long-tail cast-on method, cast
on 21 sts.

Row 1 (RS): *K1, p1; repeat from * across to
last st, k1.

Row 2 (WS): *P1, k1; repeat from * across to
last st, p1.

Row 3: *P1, k1; repeat from * across to last
st, p1.

Row 4: *K1, p1; repeat from * across to last
st, k1.

2 Repeat Rows 1–4 another six times.

3 Cast off knitwise. Weave in the ends.

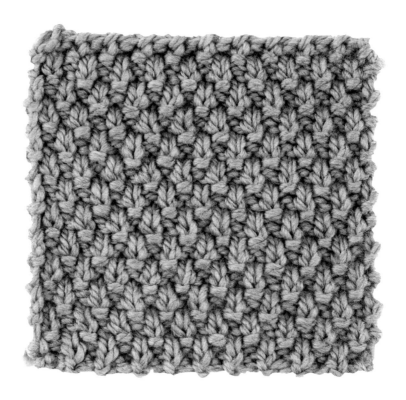

MOSS STITCH COWL

A moss stitch cowl is a must-knit cold weather accessory. Using chunky yarn, it creates a beautiful textured volume around your neck that not only looks great, but also protects you from cold winds. A cowl knitted in the round is a nice carry-on project – it is small and simple enough to work on here and there during the day, wherever you are.

BEFORE YOU BEGIN

Techniques used
Casting on, see page 14
Knitting in the round, see page 18
Casting off knitwise, see page 23
Blocking, see page 25
Weaving in ends, see page 23

Project dimensions
Finished circumference: 58.5cm (23in);
finished height: 32cm (12½in)

Tension
15 sts measure 10cm (4in). Round tension
is not crucial for this project.

Yarn
2 skeins of chunky, 100% wool, 100g (3½oz),
117m (128yd) in light grey.

Equipment
5.5m (US size 9) circular needle,
80cm (31in) long
Stitch marker
Tapestry needle

PATTERN

1 Using the long-tail cast-on method,
cast on 100 sts. Join for working in
the round, placing a stitch marker
onto the right needle to mark the
end of the round.

Rnd 1: *K1, p1; repeat from * to
the marker.
Rnd 2: *K1, p1; repeat from * to
the marker.
Rnd 3: *P1, k1; repeat from * to
the marker.
Rnd 4: *P1, k1; repeat from * to
the marker.

2 Repeat Rnds 1–4 another 20 times
or until the piece measures the
desired size.

3 Repeat Rnd 1.

4 Cast off knitwise.

Finishing

1 Block the piece.

2 Weave in the ends.

BROKEN RIB STITCH

Broken rib stitch is a variation of 1x1 rib that is broken after every four rows, which creates knit stitch columns arranged in chequerboard order. As a result, both sides of the fabric produced are identical. Broken rib is elastic widthwise and stretchy lengthwise; like most of the rib patterns, it lies flat and doesn't roll up. The knit stitch columns offset after every four rows create depth and texture, resulting in a very dense and warm fabric. The stitch has an eight-row vertical repeat but is very easy to memorise, which makes broken rib an ideal stitch pattern for big projects, such as throws, blankets, afghans and rugs.

HOW TO KNIT BROKEN RIB STITCH

Broken rib stitch has a multiple of 2 stitches. When knitting flat, work the stitch pattern over an odd number of stitches to achieve a symmetrical look at each end.

RIGHT SIDE
Row 1:

1 With the yarn at the back, insert the right needle knitwise into the next stitch on the left needle, from front to back, forming an 'x' with the needles.

2 Wrap the yarn around the right needle anticlockwise.

3 Draw the yarn through the stitch on the left needle to the front of the work to create a loop on the right needle. Drop the original stitch off the left needle (you have made one new knit stitch on the right needle).

4 Bring the yarn between the needles to the front of the work.

5 With the yarn at the front, insert the right needle purlwise into the next stitch, from back to front, forming an 'x' with the right needle at the front.

6 Wrap the yarn around the right needle anticlockwise.

7 Draw the yarn through the stitch on the left needle to the back of the work to create a loop on the right needle. Drop the original stitch off the left needle (you have made one new purl stitch on the right needle).

8 Bring the yarn between the needles to the back of the work.

Repeat Steps 1–8 until the last stitch of the row (alternate between one knit and one purl stitch).

9 With the yarn at the back, insert the right needle knitwise into the last stitch on the left needle, from front to back.

10 Wrap the yarn around the right needle anticlockwise.

11 Draw the yarn through the stitch on the left needle to the front of the work. Drop the original stitch off the left needle (this finishes the row with one knit stitch).

WRONG SIDE
Row 2:

1 With the yarn at the front, insert the right needle purlwise into the next stitch on the left needle, from back to front.

2 Wrap the yarn around the right needle anticlockwise.

3 Draw the yarn through the stitch on the left needle to the back of the work. Drop the original stitch off the left needle (you have made one new purl stitch on the right needle).

4 Bring the yarn between the needles to the back of the work.

5 Insert the right needle knitwise into the next stitch on the left needle, from front to back.

6 Wrap the yarn around the right needle anticlockwise.

7 Draw the yarn through the stitch on the left needle to the front of the work. Drop the original stitch off the left needle (you have made one new knit stitch on the right needle).

8 Bring the yarn between the needles to the front of the work.

Repeat Steps 1–8 until the last stitch of the row (alternate between one purl and one knit stitch).

9 Insert the right needle purlwise into the last stitch on the left needle, from back to front.

10 Wrap the yarn around the right needle anticlockwise.

11 Draw the yarn through the stitch on the left needle to the back of the work. Drop the original stitch off the left needle (this finishes the row with one purl stitch).

Row 3: Repeat Row 1.
Row 4: Repeat Row 2.
Row 5: Repeat Row 2.
Row 6: Repeat Row 1.
Row 7: Repeat Row 2.
Row 8: Repeat Row 1.

PRACTICE PIECE

Yarn
Super chunky, 60% baby alpaca/40% wool, 50g (1¾oz), 65m (71yd) in silver.

Needles
8mm (US size 11)

Pattern
1 Using the long-tail cast-on method, cast on 13 sts.
Row 1 (RS): *K1, p1; repeat from * across to last st, k1.
Row 2 (WS): *P1, k1; repeat from * across to last st, p1.
2 Repeat Rows 1–2 once.
3 Repeat Row 2.
4 Repeat Row 1.
5 Repeat Steps 3–4 once.
6 Repeat Steps 1–5 until the piece measures approximately 12.5cm (5in).
7 Cast off knitwise. Weave in the ends.

BROKEN RIB STITCH BABY BLANKET

Baby blankets are great projects to practise new stitches – they are small and straightforward to knit, there is no shaping involved and you don't have to worry about the exact measurements. A blanket knit in broken rib stitch will make a lovely gift for new parents. The fabric is light and stretchy – perfect for wrapping up a newborn and keeping the baby warm.

BEFORE YOU BEGIN

Techniques used
Casting on, see page 14
Slipping stitches, see page 21
Casting off knitwise, see page 23
Blocking, see page 25
Weaving in ends, see page 23

Project dimensions
Finished size (approximately):
81 x 8cm (32 x 32in)

Tension
12 sts and 16 rows measure
10 x 10cm (4 x 4in). Row tension
is not crucial for this project.

Yarn
9 skeins of super chunky,
60% baby alpaca/40% wool,
50g (1¾oz), 65m (71yd)
in rose pink.

Equipment
8mm (US size 11) needles
Tapestry needle

PATTERN

1 Using the long-tail cast-on method, cast on 101 sts. To create perfectly neat edges, the cast-on includes two selvedge stitches – one at the beginning and one at the end of each row.

Row 1 (RS): Sl 1 st purlwise, *k1, p1; repeat from * across to last 2 sts, k1, knit the last st tbl.
Row 2 (WS): Sl 1 st purlwise, *p1, k1; repeat from * across to last 2 sts, p1, knit the last st tbl.
Row 3: Repeat Row 1.
Row 4: Repeat Row 2.
Row 5: Repeat Row 2.
Row 6: Repeat Row 1.
Row 7: Repeat Row 2.
Row 8: Repeat Row 1.

2 Repeat Rows 1–8 until the blanket measures 76cm (30in), or 5cm (2 in) less than the desired size.

3 Repeat Rows 1–7 once more.

4 Cast off knitwise.

Finishing

1 Block the piece.

2 Weave in the ends.

TIP
Babies have delicate skin, so make sure to choose yarns that are made with soft, non-itchy fibres.

WAFFLE STITCH

Waffle stitch fabric resembles, as you may guess, a waffle. This visual effect is created by alternating knit and purl stitches to form textured ridges. The stitch pattern is not reversible. The wrong side of the fabric looks completely different – instead of the waffles, there are lines of knit stitch standing out against a purl background. This looks quite interesting and can easily be used for a 'public' side as well, so you can use waffle stitch to knit a lot of pieces where both sides are visible, such as blankets, scarves and double-wrap cowls. The waffle stitch lies flat, and is fairly dense and stretchy.

HOW TO KNIT WAFFLE STITCH

Waffle stitch has a multiple of 3 stitches. When knitting flat, an extra stitch is added to the end to achieve a symmetrical look at each end, so work the stitch pattern over a multiple of 3 stitches plus 1 additional stitch.

WRONG SIDE
Row 1:

1 With the yarn at the back, insert the right needle knitwise into the next stitch on the left needle, from front to back, forming an 'x' with the needles.

2 Wrap the yarn around the right needle anticlockwise.

3 Draw the yarn through the stitch on the left needle to the front of the work to create a loop on the right needle. Drop the original stitch off the left needle (you have made one new knit stitch on the right needle).

4 Bring the yarn between the needles to the front of the work.

5 With the yarn at the front, insert the right needle purlwise into the next stitch on the left needle, from back to front, forming an 'x' with the right needle at the front.

6 Wrap the yarn around the right needle anticlockwise.

7 Draw the yarn through the stitch on the left needle to the back of the work to create a loop on the right needle. Drop the original stitch off the left needle (you have made one new purl stitch on the right needle).

8 With the yarn at the front, insert the right needle purlwise into the next stitch on the left needle, from back to front.

9 Wrap the yarn around the right needle anticlockwise.

10 Draw the yarn through the stitch on the left needle to the back of the work to create a loop on the right needle. Drop the original stitch off the left needle (you have made one new purl stitch on the right needle).

11 Bring the yarn between the needles to the back of the work.

Repeat Steps 1–11 until the last stitch of the row (alternate between one knit and two purl stitches).

12 With the yarn at the back, insert the right needle knitwise into the last stitch on the left needle, from front to back.

13 Wrap the yarn around the right needle anticlockwise.

14 Draw the yarn through the stitch on the left needle to the front of the work. Drop the original stitch off the left needle (this finishes the row with one knit stitch).

RIGHT SIDE
Row 2:

1 With the yarn at the front, insert the right needle purlwise into the next stitch on the left needle, from back to front.

2 Wrap the yarn around the right needle anticlockwise.

3 Draw the yarn through the stitch on the left needle to the back of the work. Drop the original stitch off the left needle (you have made one new purl stitch on the right needle).

4 Bring the yarn between the needles to the back of the work.

5 Insert the right needle knitwise into the next stitch on the left needle, from front to back.

6 Wrap the yarn around the right needle anticlockwise.

7 Draw the yarn through the stitch on the left needle to the front of the work. Drop the original stitch off the left needle (you have made one new knit stitch on the right needle).

8 Insert the right needle knitwise into the next stitch on the left needle, from front to back.

9 Wrap the yarn around the right needle anticlockwise.

10 Draw the yarn through the stitch on the left needle to the front of the work. Drop the original stitch off the left needle (you have made one new knit stitch on the right needle).

11 Bring the yarn between the needles to the front of the work.

Repeat Steps 1–11 until the last stitch of the row (alternate between one purl and two knit stitches).

12 Insert the right needle purlwise into the last stitch on the left needle, from back to front.

13 Wrap the yarn around the right needle anticlockwise.

14 Draw the yarn through the stitch on the left needle to the back of the work. Drop the original stitch off the left needle (this finishes the row with one purl stitch).

WRONG SIDE
Row 3:

1 With the yarn at the back, insert the right needle knitwise into the next stitch on the left needle, from front to back.

2 Wrap the yarn around the right needle anticlockwise.

3 Draw the yarn through the stitch on the left needle to the front of the work. Drop the original stitch off the left needle (you have made one new knit stitch on the right needle).

Repeat Steps 1–3 until the end of the row.

RIGHT SIDE
Row 4: Repeat Row 2.

PRACTICE PIECE

Yarn

Aran, 100% cotton, 50g (1¾oz), 75m (82yd) in light grey.

Needles

4mm (US size 6)

Pattern

1 Using the long-tail cast-on method, cast on 25 sts.

Row 1 (WS): K1, *p2, k1; repeat from * across to end.

Row 2 (RS): P1, *k2, p1; repeat from * across to end.

Row 3: Knit.

Row 4: Repeat Row 2.

2 Repeat Rows 1–4 until the piece measures approximately 12.5cm (5in) or the desired size.

3 Cast off knitwise. Weave in the ends.

FRONT: The right side of the piece shows a grid of squares in 'waffle' formation.

BACK: The wrong side shows a pattern of raised lines running vertically down the fabric.

WAFFLE STITCH PHONE CASE

Protect your phone with this original phone case that is super simple to make. It is a project that you will be able to complete in an evening or two, and is perfect for leftover yarn that you might have in your stash. A stretchy fabric created by the waffle stitch will 'hug' your phone and prevent it from slipping out. It is also an ideal last-minute gift idea.

BEFORE YOU BEGIN

Techniques used
Casting on, see page 14
Casting off knitwise, see page 23
Blocking, see page 25
Invisible horizontal seam,
see page 38
Mattress stitch, see page 24
Weaving in ends, see page 23

Project dimensions
Finished width (when stretched):
7.5cm (3in); finished height:
14cm (5½in)

Tension
21 sts and 30 rows measure
10 x 10cm (4 x 4in). Row tension is
not crucial for this project.

Yarn
1 ball of aran, 100% cotton,
50g (1¾oz), 75m (82yd) in
pale pink.

Equipment
4mm (US size 6) needles
Tapestry needle

PATTERN

The front and back pieces of the phone case are knitted separately and then sewn together. For a snug fit, the finished piece should be slightly smaller than the size of your phone.

FRONT

1 Using the long-tail cast-on method, cast on 15 sts. To create perfectly neat edges, the cast-on includes two selvedge stitches – one at the beginning and one at the end of each row.

2 **Row 1 (WS):** K1, k1, *p2, k1; repeat from * across to last st, k1.
Row 2 (RS): K1, p1, *k2, p1; repeat from * across to last st, k1.
Row 3: Knit.
Row 4: Repeat Row 2.

3 Repeat Rows 1–4 until the piece measures approximately 13.5cm (5¼in).

4 Repeat Rows 1–3 once more.

5 Cast off knitwise.

BACK

Make the same as the front.

Finishing

1 Block the pieces.

2 Place the front and back pieces together, with wrong sides facing, and sew the cast-on edges together with an invisible horizontal seam. Sew the sides with mattress stitch.

3 Weave in the ends.

TIP

You can also use the wrong side of the waffle stitch as the 'public' side. Just seam the pieces together with the right sides facing inwards.

BASKETWEAVE STITCH

Basketweave stitch got its name because the fabric created using this stitch resembles the interwoven bands of a basket. The stitch looks quite elaborate, but in reality it is just a simple combination of knit and purl stitches in a specific order. Basketweave produces a textured fabric, with knit and purl 'blocks' placed in chequerboard order. The stitch has a beautiful depth to it, and it's quite engaging to watch how the pattern is formed row by row. It works well on a variety of projects, such as blankets, scarves, sweaters and washcloths.

HOW TO KNIT BASKETWEAVE STITCH

Basketweave stitch has a multiple of 8 stitches plus 5 additional stitches, and a vertical repeat of eight rows.

WRONG SIDE

Row 1:

1 With the yarn at the back, insert the right needle knitwise into the next stitch on the left needle, from front to back, forming an 'x' with the needles.

2 Wrap the yarn around the right needle anticlockwise.

3 Draw the yarn through the stitch on the left needle to the front of the work to create a loop on the right needle. Drop the original stitch off the left needle (you have made one new knit stitch on the right needle).

Repeat Steps 1–3 until the end of the row.

RIGHT SIDE

Row 2:

1 With the yarn at the back, insert the right needle knitwise into the next stitch on the left needle, from front to back.

2 Wrap the yarn around the right needle anticlockwise.

3 Draw the yarn through the stitch on the left needle to the front of the work to create a loop on the right needle. Drop the original stitch off the left needle (you have made one new knit stitch on the right needle).

4 Repeat Steps 1–3 another four times (you have five knit stitches on the right needle).

5 Bring the yarn between the needles to the front of the work.

6 With the yarn at the front, insert the right needle purlwise into the next stitch on the left needle, from back to front, forming an 'x' with the right needle at the front.

7 Wrap the yarn around the right needle anticlockwise.

8 Draw the yarn through the stitch on the left needle to the back of the work to create a loop on the right needle. Drop the original stitch off the left needle (you have made one new purl stitch on the right needle).

9 Repeat Steps 6–8 twice more (you have three purl stitches on the right needle).

10 Bring the yarn between the needles to the back of the work.

Repeat Steps 1–10 until you have five stitches on the left needle.

11 Repeat Steps 1–4 (this finishes the row with five knit stitches).

WRONG SIDE
Row 3:

1 With the yarn at the front, insert the right needle purlwise into the next stitch on the left needle, from back to front.

2 Wrap the yarn around the right needle anticlockwise.

3 Draw the yarn through the stitch on the left needle to the back of the work to create a loop on the right needle. Drop the original stitch off the left needle (you have made one new purl stitch on the right needle).

4 Repeat Steps 1–3 another four times (you have five purl stitches on the right needle).

5 Bring the yarn between the needles to the back of the work.

6 With the yarn at the back, insert the right needle knitwise into the next stitch on the left needle, from front to back.

7 Wrap the yarn around the right needle anticlockwise.

8 Draw the yarn through the stitch on the left needle to the front of the work to create a loop on the right needle. Drop the original stitch off the left needle (you have made one new knit stitch on the right needle).

9 Repeat Steps 6–8 twice more (you have three knit stitches on the right needle).

10 Bring the yarn between the needles to the front of the work.

Repeat Steps 1–10 until you have five stitches on the left needle (alternate between five purl and three knit stitches).

11 Repeat Steps 1–4 (this finishes the row with five purl stitches).

RIGHT SIDE
Row 4: Repeat Row 2.

WRONG SIDE
Row 5: Repeat Row 1.

RIGHT SIDE
Row 6:

1 With the yarn at the back, insert the right needle knitwise into the next stitch on the left needle, from front to back.

2 Wrap the yarn around the right needle anticlockwise.

3 Draw the yarn through the stitch on the left needle to the front of the work to create a loop on the right needle. Drop the original stitch off the left needle (you have made one new knit stitch on the right needle).

4 Bring the yarn between the needles to the front of the work.

5 With the yarn at the front, insert the right needle purlwise into the next stitch on the left needle, from back to front.

6 Wrap the yarn around the right needle anticlockwise.

7 Draw the yarn through the stitch on the left needle to the back of the work to create a loop on the right needle. Drop the original stitch off the left needle (you have made one new purl stitch on the right needle).

8 Repeat Steps 5–7 twice more (you have three purl stitches on the right needle).

9 Bring the yarn between the needles to the back of the work.

10 With the yarn at the back, insert the right needle knitwise into the next stitch on the left needle, from front to back.

11 Wrap the yarn around the right needle anticlockwise.

12 Draw the yarn through the stitch on the left needle to the front of the work to create a loop on the right needle. Drop the original stitch off the left needle (you have made one new knit stitch on the right needle).

13 Repeat Steps 10–12 another four times (you have five knit stitches on the right needle).

14 Repeat Steps 4–13 until you have four stitches on the left needle.

15 Repeat Steps 4–8 (you have three purl stitches on the right needle).

16 Bring the yarn between the needles to the back of the work.

17 Repeat Steps 1–3 (this finishes the row with one knit stitch).

WRONG SIDE
Row 7:
1 With the yarn at the front, insert the right needle purlwise into the next stitch on the left needle, from back to front.

2 Wrap the yarn around the right needle anticlockwise.

3 Draw the yarn through the stitch on the left needle to the back of the work. Drop the original stitch off the left needle (you have made one new purl stitch on the right needle).

4 Bring the yarn between the needles to the back of the work.

5 Insert the right needle knitwise into the next stitch on the left needle, from front to back.

6 Wrap the yarn around the right needle anticlockwise.

7 Draw the yarn through the stitch on the left needle to the front of the work to create a loop on the right needle. Drop the original stitch off the left needle (you have made one new knit stitch on the right needle).

8 Repeat Steps 5–7 twice more (you have three knit stitches).

9 Bring the yarn between the needles to the front of the work.

10 Insert the right needle purlwise into the next stitch on the left needle, from back to front.

11 Wrap the yarn around the right needle anticlockwise.

12 Draw the yarn through the stitch on the left needle to the back of the work. Drop the original stitch off the left needle (you have made one new purl stitch on the right needle).

13 Repeat Steps 10–12 another four times (you have five purl stitches on the right needle).

14 Repeat Steps 4–12 until you have four stitches on the left needle.

15 Repeat Steps 4–8 (you have three knit stitches on the right needle).

16 Bring the yarn between the needles to the front of the work.

17 Repeat Steps 1–3 (this finishes the row with one purl stitch).

RIGHT SIDE
Row 8: Repeat Row 6.

TIP

There are many variations of basketweave stitch – the look of the fabric can change drastically by modifying the proportions of the knit and purl 'blocks' that make up the pattern.

PRACTICE PIECE

Yarn
Aran, 100% cotton, 50g (1¾oz),
75m (82yd) in pale pink.

Needles
4mm (US size 6)

Pattern
1 Using the long-tail cast-on method, cast on
21 sts.
Row 1 (WS): Knit.
Row 2 (RS): K5, *p3, k5; repeat from * across
to end.

Row 3: P5, *k3, p5; repeat from * across
to end.
Row 4: Repeat Row 2.
Row 5: Repeat Row 1.
Row 6: K1, *p3, k5; repeat from * across to
last 4 sts, p3, k1.
Row 7: P1, *k3, p5; repeat from * across to
last 4 sts, k3, p1.
Row 8: Repeat Row 6.
2 Repeat Rows 1–8 another three times.
3 Cast off knitwise. Weave in the ends.

FRONT: Basketweave produces a textured
fabric, with knit and purl 'blocks' placed in
chequerboard order.

BACK: The fabric shows the stitch pattern in
reverse: the blocks of stocking stitch appear
as garter stitch and vice versa.

POT HOLDER SET

Brighten up your kitchen with this set of colourful handknit pot holders. Knitted in 100 per cent cotton, these mats are both practical and beautiful – their textured surface adds a lovely touch to the table top. You can choose contrasting colours, or create a gradient set that will complement your interior colour scheme.

BEFORE YOU BEGIN

Techniques used

Casting on, see page 14
Slipping stitches, see page 21
Casting off knitwise, see page 23
Blocking, see page 25
Weaving in ends, see page 23

Project dimensions

Finished width: 19.5cm (7¾in);
finished height: 19.5cm (7¾in)

Tension

19 sts and 29 rows measure
10 x 10cm (4 x 4in). Row tension
is not crucial for this project.

Yarn

1 ball each of aran,
100% cotton, 50g (1¾oz),
75m (82yd) in pale blue,
mid-blue and navy.

Equipment

4mm (US size 6) needles
Tapestry needle

TIP

The size of the
pot holders can be
modified by adding or
subtracting stitches. Just
remember to cast on a
number that is divisible
by a multiple of 8, plus
5 stitches for symmetry,
plus 2 additional
selvedge stitches.

PATTERN

Make one in each colour.

1 Using the long-tail cast-on method, cast on 39 sts. To create perfectly neat edges, the cast-on includes two selvedge stitches – one at the beginning and one at the end of each row.

Row 1 (WS): Sl 1 st purlwise, knit to last st, knit the last st tbl.
Row 2 (RS): Sl 1 st purlwise, k5, *p3, k5; repeat from * across to last st, knit the last st tbl.
Row 3: Sl 1 st purlwise, p5, *k3, p5; repeat from * across to last st, knit the last st tbl.
Row 4: Repeat Row 2.
Row 5: Repeat Row 1.
Row 6: Sl 1 st purlwise, k1, *p3, k5; repeat from * across to last 5 sts, p3, k1, knit the last st tbl.
Row 7: Sl 1 st purlwise, p1, *k3, p5; repeat from * across to last 5 sts, k3, p1, knit the last st tbl.
Row 8: Repeat Row 6.

2 Repeat Rows 1–8 another six times or until the piece measures 19.5cm (7¾in) or the desired size.

3 Cast off knitwise.

Finishing

1 Block the piece.

2 Weave in the ends.

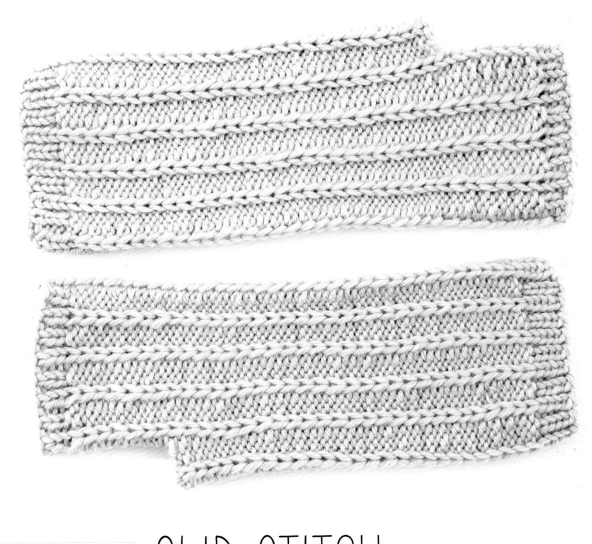

SLIP STITCH

Slip stitch is made by moving the stitch from the left needle to the right needle without actually working it. It creates the decorative effect of an elongated stitch that stands out against the simple stitch background. Slip stitch compresses the fabric vertically, because it is being pulled up directly from the lower row. Slip stitches are used in combination with numerous stitch patterns, and depending on the position of the working yarn and the way the stitches are slipped (either knitwise or purlwise), slip stitches will create different visual results. They are often used as selvedge stitches to produce a nice even edge. Slip stitches are often used in colourwork to create a beautiful mosaic effect.

HOW TO KNIT SLIP STITCH

There are many stitch patterns that use slip stitch. For this project, we are going to create the slip stitch against a reverse stocking stitch background. It has a multiple of 4 stitches. When knitting flat, an extra 3 stitches are added to the end to achieve a symmetrical look at each end, so work the stitch pattern over a multiple of 4 stitches plus 3 additional stitches. When knitting in the round, work the stitch pattern over a multiple of 4 stitches without the additional 3 stitches.

RIGHT SIDE
Row 1:

1 With the yarn at the front, insert the right needle purlwise into the next stitch, from back to front, forming an 'x' with the right needle at the front.

2 Wrap the yarn around the right needle anticlockwise.

3 Draw the yarn through the stitch on the left needle to the back of the work to create a loop on the right needle. Drop the original stitch off the left needle (you have made one new purl stitch on the right needle).

4 Repeat Steps 1–3 twice more (you have three purl stitches on the right needle).

5 Bring the yarn between the needles to the back of the work.

6 With the yarn at the back, insert the right needle purlwise into the next stitch on the left needle. Slide the stitch from the left needle to the right needle without working it (you have created one slip stitch on the right needle).

7 Bring the yarn between the needles to the front of the work.

Repeat Steps 1–7 until the last three stitches of the row (alternate between three purl stitches and one slip stitch).

Repeat Steps 1–4 (this finishes the row with three purl stitches).

WRONG SIDE
Row 2:

1 With the yarn at the back, insert the right needle knitwise into the next stitch on the left needle, from front to back, forming an 'x' with the needles.

2 Wrap the yarn around the right needle anticlockwise.

3 Draw the yarn through the stitch on the left needle to the front of the work to create a loop on the right needle. Drop the original stitch off the left needle (you have made one new knit stitch on the right needle).

4 Repeat Steps 1–3 twice more (you have three knit stitches on the right needle).

5 Bring the yarn between the needles to the front of the work.

6 With the yarn at the front, insert the right needle purlwise into the next stitch on the left needle, from back to front.

7 Wrap the yarn around the right needle anticlockwise.

8 Draw the yarn through the stitch on the left needle to the back of the work to create a loop on the right needle. Drop the original stitch off the left needle (you have made one new purl stitch on the right needle).

9 Bring the yarn between the needles to the back of the work.

Repeat Steps 1–9 until the last three stitches of the row (alternate between three knit stitches and one purl stitch).

Repeat Steps 1–4 (this finishes the row with three knit stitches).

Repeat Rows 1–2 to form the slip stitch pattern.

PRACTICE PIECE

Yarn

Aran, 55% wool/33% acrylic/ 12% cashmere, 50g (1¾oz), 90m (98yd) in mint green.

Needles

4mm (US size 6)

Pattern

1 Using the long-tail cast-on method, cast on 27 sts.

Row 1 (RS): P3, *sl 1 wyib, p3; repeat from * across to end.

Row 2 (WS): K3, *p1, k3; repeat from * across to end.

2 Repeat Rows 1–2 until the piece measures approximately 12.5cm (5in).

3 Cast off knitwise. Weave in the ends.

FRONT: The decorative effect of an elongated stitch stands out against the simple garter stitch background.

BACK: The wrong side of the fabric has a compressed effect due to the raised stitches on the right side.

SLIP STITCH MITTS

Fingerless mitts are a great accessory to keep your hands and wrists warm when the temperature drops. The slip stitches are set against a reverse stocking stitch background to create a very elegant visual effect, with beautiful textured lines running vertically along your hand. Knitted in a cashmere/wool blend, this project is a joy to knit and wear.

BEFORE YOU BEGIN

Techniques used

Casting on, see page 14
Knitting in the round, see page 18
Magic loop, see page 19
1x1 rib stitch, see page 40
Slipping stitches, see page 21
Decreasing, see page 22
Casting off knitwise, see page 23
Blocking, see page 25
Weaving in ends, see page 23

Project dimensions

Finished circumference:
16.5cm (6½in); finished height:
23cm (9in)

Tension

27 sts and 34 rounds
measure 10 x 10cm (4 x 4in).
Round tension is not crucial
for this project.

Yarn

2 balls of aran, 55% wool/
33% acrylic/12% cashmere,
50g (1¾oz), 90m (98yd)
in stone.

Equipment

4mm (US size 6) circular needle
Stitch marker
Tapestry needle

PATTERN

Make two.

1 Using the magic loop method, cast on 44 sts. Join for working in the round, placing a stitch marker onto the right needle to mark the end of the round.

2 Start with 1x1 rib:
Rnd 1: *P1, k1; repeat from * to end of rnd.

Repeat Rnd 1 (from Step 2) another four times.

3 Start the slip stitch pattern:
Rnd 1: *P3, sl 1 wyib; repeat from * to end of rnd.
Rnd 2: *P3, k1; repeat from * to end of rnd.

4 Repeat Rnds 1–2 until the piece measures approximately 18cm (7in).

5 Repeat Rnd 1 (from Step 3).

6 Make the opening for the thumb:
Next Rnd: (P3, k1) 4 times, p1, cast off 9 sts purlwise, k1, *p3, k1; repeat from * to end of rnd – 35 sts left on the needles.

7 **Rnd 1:** (P3, sl 1 wyib) 4 times, p2, sl 1 wyib, *p3, sl 1 wyib; repeat from * to end of rnd.
Rnd 2: (P3, k1) 4 times, p2, k1, *p3, k1; repeat from * to end of rnd.

8 Repeat Rnds 1–2 (from Step 7) until the piece measures approximately 21.5cm (8½in).

9 Transition from slip stitch pattern to 1x1 rib:
Next Rnd: (P1, k1) 8 times, p2tog, *k1, p1; repeat from * to last st, k1 – 34 sts left on the needles.
Next Rnd: *P1, k1; repeat from * to end of rnd.

10 Repeat last rnd twice more.

11 Cast off knitwise.

Finishing

1 Block the piece.

2 Weave in the ends.

ANDALUSIAN STITCH

Andalusian stitch is stocking stitch broken by one row of 1x1 ribbing, which creates a fabric that is covered with small 'nubs' in a grid-like pattern. The ribbing, which is repeated on every fourth row, adds texture and subtle depth to the fabric. Being a simple combination of knits and purls, this stitch pattern is very easy to memorise and quick to knit. Andalusian stitch looks different on the right and wrong sides; the fabric curls slightly at the edges, and doesn't lay perfectly flat. It is ideal for garments, such as sweaters, hats, socks and mittens.

HOW TO KNIT ANDALUSIAN STITCH

Andalusian stitch has a multiple of 2 stitches. When knitting flat, work the stitch pattern over an odd number of stitches to achieve a symmetrical look at each end.

RIGHT SIDE

Row 1:

1 With the yarn at the back, insert the right needle knitwise into the next stitch on the left needle, from front to back, forming an 'x' with the needles.

2 Wrap the yarn around the right needle anticlockwise.

3 Draw the yarn through the stitch on the left needle to the front of the work to create a loop on the right needle. Drop the original stitch off the left needle (you have made one new knit stitch on the right needle).

Repeat Steps 1–3 until the end of the row.

WRONG SIDE

Row 2:

1 With the yarn at the front, insert the right needle purlwise into the next stitch on the left needle, from back to front, forming an 'x' with the right needle at the front.

2 Wrap the yarn around the right needle anticlockwise.

3 Draw the yarn through the stitch on the left needle to the back of the work to create a loop on the right needle. Drop the original stitch off the left needle (you have made one new purl stitch on the right needle).

Repeat Steps 1–3 until the end of the row.

RIGHT SIDE

Row 3:

1 With the yarn at the back, insert the right needle knitwise into the next stitch on the left needle, from front to back.

2 Wrap the yarn around the right needle anticlockwise.

3 Draw the yarn through the stitch on the left needle to the front of the work to create a loop on the right needle. Drop the original stitch off the left needle (you have made one new knit stitch on the right needle).

4 Bring the yarn between the needles to the front of the work.

5 With the yarn at the front, insert the right needle purlwise into the next stitch on the left needle, from back to front.

6 Wrap the yarn around the right needle anticlockwise.

7 Draw the yarn through the stitch on the left needle to the back of the work to create a loop on the right needle. Drop the original stitch off the left needle (you have made one new purl stitch on the right needle).

8 Bring the yarn between the needles to the back of the work.

Repeat Steps 1–8 until the last stitch of the row (alternate between one knit and one purl stitch).

9 With the yarn at the back, insert the right needle knitwise into the last stitch on the left needle, from front to back.

10 Wrap the yarn around the right needle anticlockwise.

11 Draw the yarn through the stitch on the left needle to the front of the work. Drop the original stitch off the left needle (this finishes the row with one knit stitch).

WRONG SIDE
Row 4: Repeat Row 2.

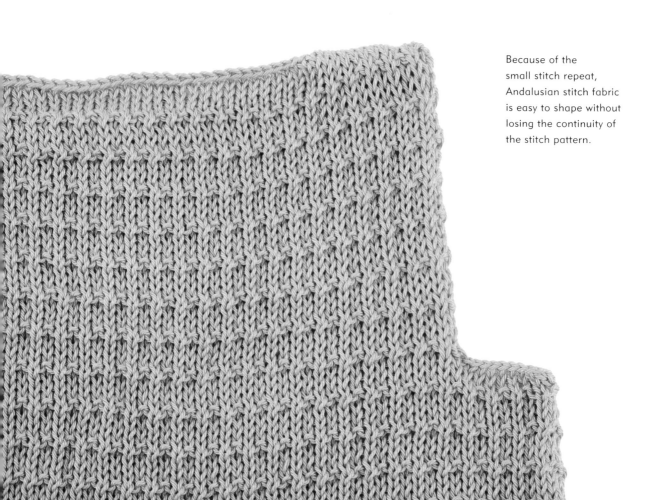

Because of the small stitch repeat, Andalusian stitch fabric is easy to shape without losing the continuity of the stitch pattern.

PRACTICE PIECE

Yarn
DK, 100% cotton, 100g (3½oz), 200m (220yd) in pale beige.

Needles
3.5mm (US size 4)

Pattern
1 Using the long-tail cast-on method, cast on 23 sts.

Row 1 (RS): Knit.

Row 2 (WS): Purl.

Row 3: *K1, p1; repeat from * across to last st, k1.

Row 4: Purl.

2 Repeat Rows 1–4 until the piece measures approximately 12.5cm (5in).

3 Cast off knitwise. Weave in the ends.

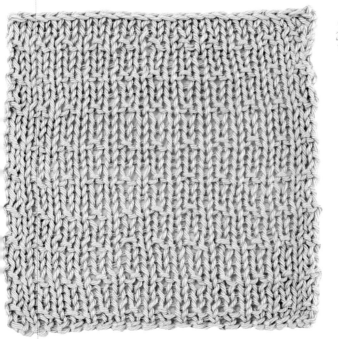

FRONT: The fabric is covered in small 'nubs' that form a grid-like pattern.

BACK: The wrong side gives the appearance of simple garter stitch.

ANDALUSIAN STITCH SUMMER TOP

This simple top is an ideal first garment project with its straightforward construction and minimal shaping. Pima cotton is a perfect fibre for summer knitting – lightweight and with a beautiful sheen, it creates a great warm weather garment. This design is easy to knit and looks wonderful in cheerful, summer colours.

BEFORE YOU BEGIN

Techniques used
How to read a pattern in multiple sizes, see page 13
Casting on, see page 14
Casting off knitwise, see page 23
Blocking, see page 25
Invisible horizontal seam, see page 38
Mattress stitch, see page 24
Weaving in ends, see page 23

Project dimensions
Small (Medium, Large)
Intended ease: 5cm (2in)
Finished bust measurement (approximately): 81 (96.5, 112) cm/ 32 (38, 44) in; finished length: 58.5 (61, 65) cm/ 23 (24, 25½) in.

Tension
20 sts and 24 rows measure 10 x 10cm (4 x 4in) when stretched. Row tension is not crucial for this project.

Yarn
3 (4, 4) skeins of DK, 100% cotton, 100g (3½oz), 200m (220yd) in coral.

Equipment
3.5mm (US size 4) needles
Tapestry needle

PATTERN

FRONT

1 Using the long-tail cast-on method, cast on 81 (95, 109) sts. To create perfectly neat edges, the cast-on includes two selvedge stitches – one at the beginning and one at the end of each row.

Row 1 (RS): Knit.
Row 2 (WS): Purl.
Row 3: *K1, p1; repeat from * across to last st, k1.
Row 4: Purl.

2 Repeat Rows 1–4 (from Step 1) until the piece measures approximately 40 (41.5, 43) cm/ 15½ (16¼, 17) in.

3 Shape the armholes as follows:
Next Row (RS): Cast off 8 (10, 12) sts knitwise, knit to end – 73 (85, 97) sts left on the needles.
Next Row (WS): Cast off 8 (10, 12) sts purlwise, purl to end – 65 (75, 85) sts left on the needles.

4 Continue in pattern:
Next Row (RS): *K1, p1; repeat from * across to last st, k1.
Next Row (WS): Purl.

5 **Row 1 (RS):** Knit.
Row 2 (WS): Purl.
Row 3: *K1, p1; repeat from * across to last st, k1.
Row 4: Purl.

6 Repeat Rows 1–4 (from Step 5) until the armhole measures approximately 18 (19, 20) cm/ 7 (7½, 8) in.

7 Cast off knitwise.

BACK
Make the same as the front.

Finishing

1 Block the pieces.

2 Lay the pieces with wrong sides together and sew the shoulders with an invisible horizontal seam.

3 Sew the sides up to the armhole opening with mattress stitch.

4 Weave in the ends.

TIP

Pima cotton yarn can be slippery to work with. Try using wooden or bamboo needles, instead of metal ones, to prevent the stitches from slipping.

OBLIQUE RIB STITCH

Oblique rib stitch is a type of broken rib stitch that forms a diagonal ridge running across the fabric. The pattern is reversible and creates a reasonably firm piece of fabric that lies flat and doesn't curl at the edges – ideal for interior items and accessories. This stitch is formed by alternating knits and purls, just like all ribbing stitches. However, it is much less obvious and is more complicated than other rib variations. Because of the diagonal line created, patterns that use oblique rib stitch have less horizontal stretch than other rib stitch fabrics.

HOW TO KNIT OBLIQUE RIB STITCH

Oblique rib stitch has a multiple of 4 stitches, and a vertical repeat of four rows.

WRONG SIDE
Row 1:

1 With the yarn at the back, insert the right needle knitwise into the next stitch on the left needle, from front to back, forming an 'x' with the needles.

2 Wrap the yarn around the right needle anticlockwise.

3 Draw the yarn through the stitch on the left needle to the front of the work to create a loop on the right needle. Drop the original stitch off the left needle (you have made one new knit stitch on the right needle).

4 Repeat Steps 1–3 once more (you have two knit stitches on the right needle).

5 Bring the yarn between the needles to the front of the work.

6 With the yarn at the front, insert the right needle purlwise into the next stitch on the left needle, from back to front, forming an 'x' with the right needle at the front.

7 Wrap the yarn around the right needle anticlockwise.

8 Draw the yarn through the stitch on the left needle to the back of the work to create a loop on the right needle. Drop the original stitch off the left needle (you have made one new purl stitch on the right needle).

9 Repeat Steps 6–8 once more (you have two purl stitches on the right needle).

10 Bring the yarn between the needles to the back of the work.

Repeat Steps 1–10 until the end of the row (alternate between two knit and two purl stitches).

RIGHT SIDE
Row 2:

1 With the yarn at the back, insert the right needle knitwise into the next stitch on the left needle, from front to back, forming an 'x' with the needles.

2 Wrap the yarn around the right needle anticlockwise.

3 Draw the yarn through the stitch on the left needle to the front of the work to create a loop on the right needle. Drop the original stitch off the left needle (you have made one new knit stitch on the right needle).

4 Bring the yarn between the needles to the front of the work.

5 Insert the right needle purlwise into the next stitch on the left needle, from back to front.

6 Wrap the yarn around the right needle anticlockwise.

7 Draw the yarn through the stitch on the left needle to the back of the work. Drop the original stitch off the left needle (you have made one new purl stitch on the right needle).

8 Repeat Steps 5–7 once more (you have one more purl stitch).

9 Bring the yarn between the needles to the back of the work.

10 Insert the right needle knitwise into the next stitch on the left needle, from front to back.

11 Wrap the yarn around the right needle anticlockwise.

12 Draw the yarn through the stitch on the left needle to the front of the work. Drop the original stitch off the left needle (you have made one new knit stitch on the right needle).

13 Repeat Steps 10–12 once more (you have one more knit stitch).

14 Repeat Steps 4–13 until the last three stitches of the row.

15 Repeat Steps 4–12.

WRONG SIDE
Row 3:

1 With the yarn at the front, insert the right needle purlwise into the next stitch on the left needle, from back to front.

2 Wrap the yarn around the right needle anticlockwise.

3 Draw the yarn through the stitch on the left needle to the back of the work. Drop the original stitch off the left needle (you have made one new purl stitch on the right needle).

4 Repeat the Steps 1–3 once more (you have one more purl stitch).

5 Bring the yarn between the needles to the back of the work.

6 Insert the right needle knitwise into the next stitch on the left needle, from front to back.

7 Wrap the yarn around the right needle anticlockwise.

8 Draw the yarn through the stitch on the left needle to the front of the work. Drop the stitch off the left needle (you have made one new knit stitch on the right needle).

9 Repeat Steps 6–8 once more (you have one more knit stitch).

10 Bring the yarn between the needles to the front of the work.

Repeat Steps 1–10 until the end of the row (alternate between two purl and two knit stitches).

RIGHT SIDE
Row 4:

1 With the yarn at the front, insert the right needle purlwise into the next stitch on the left needle, from back to front.

2 Wrap the yarn around the right needle anticlockwise.

3 Draw the yarn through the stitch on the left needle to the back of the work. Drop the original stitch off the left needle (you have made one new purl stitch on the right needle).

4 Bring the yarn between the needles to the back of the work.

5 Insert the right needle knitwise into the next stitch on the left needle, from front to back.

6 Wrap the yarn around the right needle anticlockwise.

7 Draw the yarn through the stitch on the left needle to the front of the work. Drop the original stitch off the left needle (you have made one new knit stitch on the right needle).

8 Repeat Steps 5–7 once more (you have one more knit stitch).

9 Bring the yarn between the needles to the front of the work.

10 Insert the right needle purlwise into the next stitch on the left needle, from back to front.

11 Wrap the yarn around the right needle anticlockwise.

12 Draw the yarn through the stitch on the left needle to the back of the work. Drop the original stitch off the left needle (you have made one new purl stitch on the right needle).

13 Repeat Steps 10–12 once more (you have one more purl stitch).

14 Repeat Steps 4–13 until the last three stitches of the row.

15 Repeat Steps 4–12.

102

PRACTICE PIECE

Yarn
Aran, 100% cotton, 50g (1¾oz),
75m (82yd) in mint green.

Needles
3.5mm (US size 4)

Pattern
1 Using the long-tail cast-on method,
cast on 20 sts.
Row 1 (WS): *K2, p2; repeat from *
across to end.
Row 2 (RS): K1, *p2, k2; repeat from
* across to last 3 sts, p2, k1.
Row 3: *P2, k2; repeat from * across
to end.
Row 4: P1, *k2, p2; repeat from *
across to last 3 sts, k2, p1.
2 Repeat Rows 1–4 until the piece
measures approximately 12.5cm (5in)
or the desired size.
3 Cast off knitwise. Weave in the ends.

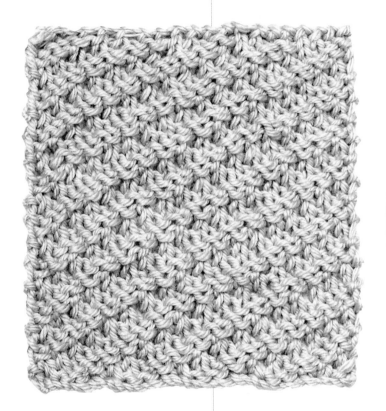

OBLIQUE RIB TOTE

This knitted tote is perfect for storing your current projects or yarn, and is a great accessory to take to summer markets and fill with freshly picked flowers. The tote is knitted in oblique rib stitch, using 100 per cent cotton, which will help the bag to keep its shape for many seasons.

BEFORE YOU BEGIN

Techniques used
Casting on, see page 14
Casting off, see page 23
Blocking, see page 25
Mattress stitch, see pages 24 and 106
Weaving in ends, see page 23

Project dimensions
Finished width: 32cm (12½in); finished height: 34.5cm (13½in)

Tension
18 sts and 30 rows measure 10 x 10cm (4 x 4in) when slightly stretched. Row tension is not crucial for this project.

Yarn
Aran, 100% cotton, 50g (1¾oz), 75m (82yd); 4 balls in emerald green, 1 ball in mint green.

Equipment
3.5mm (US size 4) needles; 3.25mm (US size 3) needles
Tapestry needle

PATTERN

Note: Knit the body of the bag flat and then fold it in half and seam the sides to create the tote.

1 Using 3.5mm (US size 4) needles and the long-tail cast-on method, cast on 56 sts.

Row 1 (WS): P1, *k2, p2; repeat from * across to last st, p1.
Row 2 (RS): K1, k1, *p2, k2; repeat from * across to last 3 sts, p2, k1, k1.
Row 3: P1, *p2, k2; repeat from * across to last st, p1.
Row 4: K1, p1, *k2, p2; repeat from * across to last 4 sts, k2, p1, k1.

2 Repeat Rows 1–4 until the piece measures approximately 67.5cm (26½in).

3 Repeat Rows 1–3 once more.

4 Cast off in the pattern of Row 4.

Handles (make two)

Note: Knit the handles separately and in a different stitch pattern (seed stitch) for additional texture contrast.

1 Using 3.25mm (US size 3) needles and the long-tail cast-on method, cast on 9 sts.

Row 1 (RS): K1, *p1, k1; repeat from * across to end.
Row 2 (WS): Repeat Row 1.

2 Repeat Rows 1–2 until the piece measures 56cm (22in). Cast off in pattern as follows:

3 K2 – you have two stitches on your right needle.

4 Insert left needle from left to right into the front of second st; pull it over the first st and slip it off the needle. You have cast off one stitch (one stitch remains on right needle).

5 Purl 1 stitch and repeat Step 4. Repeat.

6 Knit 1 stitch and repeat Step 4. Repeat.

7 Repeat Steps 5 and 6 across the row until you have two stitches on your left needle.

8 Repeat Step 5. You have one stitch left (on right hand needle), cut the yarn and pull the tail through the last stitch, tighten to secure the work.

Finishing

1 Block all the pieces.

2 Fold the body of the bag in half with wrong sides together. With right side facing, sew the side edges together with mattress stitch. Sew the handles to the inside of the bag, approximately 4cm (1½in) from the bag's edge. Weave in the ends.

HURDLE RIB STITCH

Hurdle rib stitch is a combination of garter stitch and 1x1 ribbing, which makes it engaging to knit because you switch the stitch placement every two rows. The fabric created is striking – very rich in texture and volume; thick and not too loose. Both sides of the hurdle rib are identical, covered with horizontal ridges (created by two rows of garter stitch) and vertical stitch columns (created by two rows of ribbing). As the hurdle rib stays perfectly flat, its edges do not require any special trimming, which makes this stitch ideal for accessories and interior pieces with raw edges, such as blankets, rugs, coasters and decorative wall hangings.

HOW TO KNIT HURDLE RIB STITCH

Hurdle rib stitch has a multiple of 2 stitches. When knitting flat, work the stitch pattern over an odd number of stitches to achieve a symmetrical look at each end.

RIGHT SIDE
Row 1:

1 With the yarn at the back, insert the right needle knitwise into the next stitch on the left needle, from front to back, forming an 'x' with the needles.

2 Wrap the yarn around the right needle anticlockwise.

3 Draw the yarn through the stitch on the left needle to the front of the work to create a loop on the right needle. Drop the original stitch off the left needle (you have made one new knit stitch on the right needle).

Repeat Steps 1–3 until the end of the row.

WRONG SIDE
Row 2: Repeat Row 1.

RIGHT SIDE
Row 3:

1 With the yarn at the back, insert the right needle knitwise into the next stitch on the left needle, from front to back.

2 Wrap the yarn around the right needle anticlockwise.

3 Draw the yarn through the stitch on the left needle to the front of the work to create a loop on the right needle. Drop the original stitch off the left needle (you have made one new knit stitch on the right needle).

4 Bring the yarn between the needles to the front of the work.

5 With the yarn at the front, insert the right needle purlwise into the next stitch on the left needle, from back to front, forming an 'x' with the right needle at the front.

6 Wrap the yarn around the right needle anticlockwise.

7 Draw the yarn through the stitch on the left needle to the back of the work to create a loop on the right needle. Drop the original stitch off the left needle (you have made one new purl stitch on the right needle).

8 Bring the yarn between the needles to the back of the work.

Repeat Steps 1–8 until the last stitch of the row (alternate between one knit and one purl stitch).

9 With the yarn at the back, insert the right needle knitwise into the last stitch on the left needle, from front to back.

10 Wrap the yarn around the right needle anticlockwise.

11 Draw the yarn through the stitch on the left needle to the front of the work to create a loop on the right needle. Drop the original stitch off the left needle (this finishes the row with one knit stitch).

WRONG SIDE
Row 4:

1 With the yarn at the front, insert the right needle purlwise into the next stitch on the left needle, from back to front.

2 Wrap the yarn around the right needle anticlockwise.

3 Draw the yarn through the stitch on the left needle to the back of the work to create a loop on the right needle. Drop the original stitch off the left needle (you have made one new purl stitch on the right needle).

4 Bring the yarn between the needles to the back of the work.

5 With the yarn at the back, insert the right needle knitwise into the next stitch on the left needle, from front to back.

6 Wrap the yarn around the right needle anticlockwise.

7 Draw the yarn through the stitch on the left needle to the front of the work to create a stitch on the right needle. Drop the original stitch off the left needle (you have made one new knit stitch on the right needle).

8 Bring the yarn between the needles to the front of the work.

Repeat Steps 1–8 until the last stitch of the row (alternate between one knit and one purl stitch).

9 With the yarn at the front, insert the right needle purlwise into the last stitch on the left needle, from back to front.

10 Wrap the yarn around the right needle anticlockwise.

11 Draw the yarn through the stitch on the left needle to the back of the work to create a loop on the right needle. Drop the stitch off the left needle (this finishes the row with one purl stitch).

PRACTICE PIECE

Yarn
Super chunky, 100% wool, 250g (8¾oz),
112.5m (123yd) in lilac.

Needles
10mm (US size 15)

Pattern
1 Using the long-tail cast-on method, cast on
11 sts.
Row 1 (RS): Knit.
Row 2 (WS): Knit.
Row 3: *K1, p1; repeat from * across to last st, k1.
Row 4: *P1, k1; repeat from * across to last st, p1.
2 Repeat Rows 1–4 twice more.
3 Repeat Rows 1–2 once more.
4 Cast off knitwise. Weave in ends.

TIP

You can experiment with hurdle stitch by changing the number of rows in each vertical repeat. Try eight rows (four rows of knit and four rows of 1x1 ribbing) instead of the four rows (two rows of knit and two rows of 1x1 ribbing) in the original pattern, and see how it changes the look of the fabric.

HURDLE RIB STITCH BED BLANKET

Personalise your home with a handknit one-of-a-kind throw. Super chunky Peruvian highland wool creates a deliciously soft and cosy fabric that you can cuddle up with on cool nights. This reversible stitch pattern is easy to knit and the texture created is the perfect addition to any interior.

BEFORE YOU BEGIN

Techniques used

Casting on, see page 14

Knitting flat with circular needles, see page 20

Slipping stitches, see page 21

Casting off knitwise, see page 23

Blocking, see page 25

Weaving in ends, see page 23

Project dimensions

Finished width: 114cm (45in);
finished height: 142cm (56 in)

Tension

7.5 sts measure 10cm (4in). Row tension is not crucial for this project.

Yarn

5 skeins of super chunky, 100% wool, 250g (8¾oz), 112.5m (123yd) in fawn.

Equipment

10mm (US size 15) circular needle, 80cm (31in) long

Tapestry needle

Note: The circular needle is used for flat knitting (in rows). It will allow you to accommodate the number of stitches required.

PATTERN

1 Using the long-tail cast-on method, cast on 69 sts. To create perfectly neat edges, the cast-on includes two selvedge stitches – one at the beginning and one at the end of each row.

2 **Set-up Row 1 (RS):** Sl 1 st purlwise wyib, knit to last st, p1.
Set-up Row 2 (WS): Sl 1 st purlwise wyib, knit to last st, p1.

3 **Row 1 (RS):** Sl 1 st purlwise wyib, knit to last st, p1.
Row 2 (WS): Sl 1 st purlwise wyib, knit to last st, p1.
Row 3: Sl 1 st purlwise wyib, *k1, p1; repeat from * across to last 2 sts, k1, p1.
Row 4: Sl 1 st purlwise wyib, *p1, k1; repeat from * across to last 2 sts, p1, p1.

4 Repeat Rows 1–4 another 42 times or until the piece measures approximately 142cm (56in) or the desired size.

5 Repeat Set-up Rows 1–2 twice more.

6 Cast off knitwise.

Finishing

1 Block the piece.

2 Weave in the ends.

1X1 GARTER RIB STITCH

1x1 garter rib stitch is a variation of the classic 1x1 ribbing and shares its qualities – it is very stretchy; the fabric produced lies flat and doesn't roll; and the two-stitch pattern repeat is easy to memorise. Unlike 1x1 rib, garter rib looks completely different on the right and wrong sides of the knitted piece. One side has V-shaped columns running vertically along the fabric; the other side is more textured and covered in little 'bumps'. The detail of the stitch makes it perfect for projects where both sides are visible. Double-wrap cowls, folded sleeve cuffs and neckbands all work well in 1x1 garter rib.

HOW TO KNIT 1X1 GARTER RIB STITCH

1x1 garter rib stitch has a multiple of 2 stitches. When knitting flat, work the stitch pattern over an odd number of stitches to achieve a symmetrical look at each end.

RIGHT SIDE
Row 1:

1 With the yarn at the back, insert the right needle knitwise into the next stitch on the left needle, from front to back, forming an 'x' with the needles.

2 Wrap the yarn around the right needle anticlockwise.

3 Draw the yarn through the stitch on the left needle to the front of the work to create a loop on the right needle. Drop the original stitch off the left needle (you have made one new knit stitch on the right needle).

4 Bring the yarn between the needles to the front of the work.

5 With the yarn at the front, insert the right needle purlwise into the next stitch on the left needle, from back to front, forming an 'x' with the right needle at the front.

6 Wrap the yarn around the right needle anticlockwise.

7 Draw the yarn through the stitch on the left needle to the back of the work. Drop the original stitch off the left needle.

8 Bring the yarn to the back.

Repeat Steps 1–8 until the last stitch of the row.

9 With the yarn at the back, insert the right needle knitwise into the last stitch on the left needle, from front to back.

10 Wrap the yarn around the right needle anticlockwise.

11 Draw the yarn through the stitch on the left needle to the front of the work. Drop the original stitch off the left needle (this finishes the row with one knit stitch).

WRONG SIDE
Row 2:

1 With the yarn at the back, insert the right needle knitwise into the next stitch on the left needle, from front to back.

2 Wrap the yarn around the right needle anticlockwise.

3 Draw the yarn through the stitch on the left needle to the front of the work to create a loop on the right needle. Drop the original stitch off the left needle (you have made one new knit stitch on the right needle).

Repeat Steps 1–3 to the end of the row.

PRACTICE PIECE

Yarn
Super chunky, 65% wool/35% alpaca, 100g (3½oz), 90m (98yd) in light brown.

Needles
6.5mm (US size 10)

Pattern
1 Using the long-tail cast-on method, cast on 15 sts.
Row 1 (RS): K1, *p1, k1; repeat from * across to end.
Row 2 (WS): Knit.
2 Repeat Rows 1–2 until the piece measures approximately 12cm (4¾in) or the desired size.
3 Cast off in pattern. Weave in the ends.

FRONT: The right side has straight V-shaped columns running vertically along the fabric.

BACK: The wrong side is more textured and covered in little 'bumps'.

1X1 GARTER RIB
DOUBLE-WRAP COWL

A double-wrap cowl knit in an alpaca/wool blend will feel warm and luxurious against your neck and keep you cosy in any weather. The voluminous effect is created by two layers of fabric, and the different sides of the same stitch pattern produce a beautiful contrast of textures.

BEFORE YOU BEGIN

Techniques used

Casting on, see page 14
Knitting in the round, see page 18
Casting off, see pages 23 and 44
Blocking, see page 25
Weaving in ends, see page 23

Project dimensions

Finished circumference:
142cm (56in); finished
height: 35.5cm (14in)

Tension

12 sts and 17 rounds
measure 10 x 10cm (4 x 4in).
Round tension is not crucial
for this project.

Yarn

5 balls of super chunky,
65% wool/35% alpaca,
100g (3½oz), 90m (98yd)
in lilac-grey.

Equipment

6.5mm (US size 10) needles
Stitch marker
Tapestry needle

PATTERN

1 Using the long-tail cast-on method,
cast on 162 sts. Join for working in
the round, placing a stitch marker
onto the right needle to mark the
end of the round.

Rnd 1: *K1, p1; repeat from * to
the marker.
Rnd 2: Knit to the marker.

2 Repeat Rnds 1–2 until the piece
measures approximately 35.5cm
(14in) or the desired size.

3 Cast off in pattern following the
instructions on page 44.

Finishing

1 Block the piece.

2 Weave in the ends.

3X1 SEED RIB STITCH

Seed rib stitch is one of the endless combinations that you can knit once you have the hang of the basic stitches. It is the perfect example of how adding one stitch can completely change the look of the fabric produced. Seed rib stitch is made up of stocking stitch columns that stand out against a background of seed stitch. The result is a very dense fabric that still has some elasticity to it, which makes it suitable for cold weather accessories and garments. It is a great alternative to classic ribbing, but keep in mind that unlike classic ribbing, the seed rib isn't reversible.

HOW TO KNIT 3X1 SEED RIB STITCH

3x1 seed rib stitch has a multiple of 4 stitches. When knitting flat, an extra 3 stitches are added to the end to achieve a symmetrical look at each end, so work the stitch pattern over a multiple of 4 stitches plus 3 additional stitches. When knitting in the round, work the stitch pattern over a multiple of 4 stitches without the additional 3 stitches.

RIGHT SIDE
Row 1:

1 With the yarn at the back, insert the right needle knitwise into the next stitch on the left needle, from front to back, forming an 'x' with the needles.

2 Wrap the yarn around the right needle anticlockwise.

3 Draw the yarn through the stitch on the left needle to the front of the work to create a loop on the right needle. Drop the original stitch off the left needle (you have made one new knit stitch on the right needle).

4 Bring the yarn between the needles to the front of the work.

5 With the yarn at the front, insert the right needle purlwise into the next stitch, from back to front, forming an 'x' with the right needle at the front.

6 Wrap the yarn around the right needle anticlockwise.

7 Draw the yarn through the stitch on the left needle to the back of the work to create a loop on the right needle. Drop the original stitch off the left needle (you have made one new purl stitch on the right needle).

8 Bring the yarn between the needles to the back of the work.

9 With the yarn at the back, insert the right needle knitwise into the next stitch on the left needle, from front to back.

10 Wrap the yarn around the right needle anticlockwise.

11 Draw the yarn through the stitch on the left needle to the front of the work to create a loop on the right needle. Drop the original stitch off the left needle (you have made one new knit stitch on the right needle).

12 With the yarn at the back, insert the right needle knitwise into the next stitch on the left needle, from front to back.

13 Wrap the yarn around the right needle anticlockwise.

14 Draw the yarn through the stitch on the left needle to the front of the work to create a loop on the right needle. Drop the original stitch off the left needle (you have made one new knit stitch on the right needle).

Repeat Steps 1–14 until the last three stitches of the row.

Repeat Steps 1–11 once more (alternate between three stitches of seed pattern and one stocking stitch).

WRONG SIDE
Row 2:
1 With the yarn at the back, insert the right needle knitwise into the next stitch on the left needle, from front to back.

2 Wrap the yarn around the right needle anticlockwise.

3 Draw the yarn through the stitch on the left needle to the front of the work to create a loop on the right needle. Drop the original stitch off the left needle (you have made one new knit stitch on the right needle).

4 Bring the yarn between the needles to the front of the work.

5 With the yarn at the front, insert the right needle purlwise into the next stitch on the left needle, from back to front.

6 Wrap the yarn around the right needle anticlockwise.

7 Draw the yarn through the stitch on the left needle to the back of the work to create a loop on the right needle. Drop the original stitch off the left needle (you have made one new purl stitch on the right needle).

8 Bring the yarn between the needles to the back of the work.

Repeat Steps 1–8 until the last stitch of the row (alternate between one knit and one purl stitch).

9 With the yarn at the back, insert the right needle knitwise into the last stitch on the left needle, from front to back.

10 Wrap the yarn around the right needle anticlockwise.

11 Draw the yarn through the stitch on the left needle to the front of the work to create a loop on the right needle. Drop the original stitch off the left needle (this finishes the row with one knit stitch).

PRACTICE PIECE

Yarn
Super chunky, 65% wool/35% alpaca, 100g (3½oz), 75m (82yd) in sage green.

Needles
5.5m (US size 9)

Pattern
1 Using the long-tail cast-on method, cast on 23 sts.
Row 1 (RS): *K1, p1, k2; repeat from * across to last 3 sts, k1, p1, k1.
Row 2 (WS): *K1, p1; repeat from * across to last st, k1.
2 Repeat Rows 1–2 until the piece measures approximately 12.5cm (5in).
3 Cast off in pattern. Weave in the ends.

3X1 SEED RIB STITCH POM-POM HAT

This textured hat is a great way to practise your knitting skills while making something stylish and wearable at the end. The project combines two types of ribbing – the classic 1x1 rib and seed rib, which creates a beautiful textural contrast. And to make things more fun, you can add a cute pom-pom at the top as the perfect finishing touch.

BEFORE YOU BEGIN

Techniques used
Casting on, see page 14
Knitting in the round, see page 18
Decreasing, see page 22
Making a pom-pom, see page 124
Weaving in ends, see page 23
Blocking, see page 25

Project dimensions
Finished circumference: 57cm (22½in); finished height (with hem unfolded): 32cm (12½in)

Tension
9 sts and 20 rounds measure 10 x 10cm (4 x 4in). Round tension is not crucial for this project.

Yarn
1 skein of aran, 100% wool, 100g (3½oz), 202m (220yd) in cream HELD DOUBLE (see step 1).

Equipment
8mm (US size 11) circular needle, 40.5cm (16in) long
Stitch marker
Tapestry needle
Pom-pom maker

PATTERN

1 Using the long-tail cast-on method and holding both ends of the yarn together, cast on 52 sts. (To prevent the yarn from tangling, put the ball in a plastic bag, cut two holes and feed one end through each hole.) Join for working in the round, placing a stitch marker onto the right needle to mark the end of the round.

Rnd 1: *P1, k1; repeat from * to the end of the rnd.

2 Repeat Rnd 1 until the piece measures approximately 18cm (7in).

3 Start the seed rib pattern:
Rnd 1: *K1, p1, k2; repeat from * to the end of the rnd.
Rnd 2: *P1, k1; repeat from * to the end of the rnd.

4 Repeat Rnds 1–2 of the seed rib pattern (from Step 3) until the piece measures approximately 30cm (11¾in).

5 Start the decrease rounds:
Dec Rnd 1: *P3tog, k1; repeat from * to the end of the rnd – 26 sts left on the needles.
Next Rnd: Knit.
Dec Rnd 2: *K2tog; repeat from * to the end of the rnd – 13 sts left on the needles.
Dec Rnd 3: *K2tog; repeat from * to last st, k1 – 7 sts left on the needles.

6 Cut the yarn, leaving a tail approximately 25.5cm (10in) long. Thread the tail through a tapestry needle and draw it through the remaining 7 sts, slipping them off the needle one by one. Pull tightly to gather the stitches together and 'close' the top of the hat. Weave in the tail on the inside.

7 Make a pom-pom and attach it to the crown of the hat by threading the yarn tails of the pom-pom through to the inside of the hat. Tie a knot to secure the pom-pom in place, then cut the tails.

Finishing

1 Block the piece and weave in the ends.

Pom-Pom Tutorial

Step 1 Open the 'arms' of the pom-pom maker and wrap the yarn around one open arm. The more you wrap, the fuller your pom-pom will be.

Step 2 Repeat Step 1 and wrap the yarn around the other arm. Close both arms.

Step 3 Use a pair of sharp scissors to cut the yarn wrapped around the arms.

Step 4 Wrap a 25.5cm (10in) piece of yarn around the middle of the pom-pom and tie a tight double knot. Leave the ends of the knot long and use them to attach the pom-pom to your project later.

Step 5 Open the arms of the pom-pom maker and take the pom-pom out. Using the scissors, trim the pom-pom until you achieve the desired shape.

YARNS USED IN THE LESSONS

LESSON 1 – Garter stitch
Drops Andes,
65% wool/35% alpaca,
100g (3½oz), 90m (98yd).
Practice piece
1 ball in 8465
Scarf
4 balls in 4276

LESSON 2 – Stocking stitch
Cascade Lana Grande,
100% wool, 100g (3½oz),
80m (87½yd).
Practice piece
1 ball in 6010
Cushion cover
3 balls in 6043

LESSON 3 – 1x1 rib stitch
Cascade 128 Superwash,
100% wool, 100g (3½oz),
117m (128yd).
Practice piece
1 skein in 232
Hat
2 skeins in 247

LESSON 4 – 2x2 rib stitch
Drops Nepal,
65% wool/35% alpaca,
50g (1¾oz), 75m (82yd).
Practice piece
1 ball in 8907
Leg warmers
4 balls in 500

LESSON 5 – Seed stitch
Debbie Bliss Cashmerino Aran,
55% wool/33% acrylic/
12% cashmere, 50g (1¾oz),
90m (98yd).
Practice piece
1 ball in 102
Headband
1 ball in 78

LESSON 6 – Moss stitch
Cascade 128 Superwash,
100% wool, 100g (3½oz),
117m (128yd).
Practice piece
1 skein in 1926
Cowl
2 skeins in 875

LESSON 7 – Broken rib stitch
Debbie Bliss Paloma,
60% baby alpaca/40% wool,
50g (1¾oz), 65m (71yd).
Practice piece
1 skein in 24
Baby blanket
9 skeins in 41

LESSON 8 – Waffle stitch
Drops Paris, 100% cotton,
50g (1¾oz), 75m (82yd).
Practice piece
1 ball in 23
Phone case
1 ball in 58

LESSON 9 – Basketweave stitch
Drops Paris, 100% cotton,
50g (1¾oz), 75m (82yd).
Practice piece
1 ball in 110
Pot holder set
1 ball each in 100, 101 and 102

LESSON 10 – Slip stitch
Debbie Bliss Cashmerino Aran,
55% wool/33% acrylic/
12% cashmere, 50g (1¾oz),
90m (98yd).
Practice piece
1 ball in 81
Mitts
2 balls in 27

LESSON 11 – Andalusian stitch
Cascade Ultra Pima, 100% cotton,
100g (3½oz), 200m (220yd).
Practice piece
1 skein in 3719
Summer top
3 (4, 4) skeins in 3752

LESSON 12 – Oblique rib stitch
Drops Paris, 100% cotton,
50g (1¾oz), 75m (82yd).
Practice piece
1 ball in 11
Tote
4 balls in 11
1 ball in 21

LESSON 13 – Hurdle rib stitch
Cascade Magnum, 100% wool,
250g (8¾oz), 112.5m (123yd).
Practice piece
1 skein in 8242
Bed blanket
5 skeins in 8012

**LESSON 14 – 1x1 garter
rib stitch**
Drops Andes, 65% wool/
35% alpaca, 100g (3½oz),
90m (98yd).
Practice piece
1 ball in 5310
Double-wrap cowl
5 balls in 4010

LESSON 15 – 3x1 seed rib stitch
Practice piece
Drops Nepal, 65% wool/
35% alpaca, 100g (3½oz),
75m (82yd). 1 ball in 206.
Pom-pom hat
YOTH Father, 100% wool,
100g (3½oz), 202m (220yd).
1 skein in Hazelnut.

ABBREVIATIONS

dec	decrease
k	knit
k2tog	knit 2 together
p	purl
p2tog	purl 2 together
rnd	round
RS	right side
sl	slip
st(s)	stitch(es)
tbl	through back loop
WS	wrong side
wyib	with yarn in back

RESOURCES

WEBSITES:

craftsy.com
craftyarncouncil.com
giftofknitting.com
ravelry.com
TECHknitting.blogspot.com

BOOKS:

The Principles of Knitting, June Hemmons Hiatt
A Treasury of Knitting Patterns, Barbara G. Walker
Second Treasury of Knitting Patterns, Barbara G. Walker
Vogue Knitting: The Ultimate Knitting Book, Vogue
Vogue Knitting Stitchionary: The Ultimate Stitch Dictionary: Knit and Purl v. 1, Trisha Malcolm

INDEX

ACKNOWLEDGEMENTS

To my dear Granny Eugenia and Granny Lidia. Thank you for your unconditional love.

I would like to express my gratitude to a wonderful knitting community for their constant support and encouragement. Thank you for knitting my designs, your beautiful letters and kind comments. This book would never have happened without you!

I would like to thank my editor Charlotte Frost for guiding me through the whole process, offering comments, expertise and encouragement.

Last but not least I would love to thank my husband for believing in me.

The publisher would like to thank the following for their help in making this book:

Alina Schneider, for her beautiful designs and clear and coherent patterns and instructions.

Many thanks to Debbie Bliss and The Designer Yarns Group, Cascade Yarns® (www.cascadeyarns.com) and DROPS Design (www.garnstudio.com) for supplying the yarn for the projects.

Thank you to our photographer Simon Pask, and our models Virginia Lee, Georgina Terry and Emma Brace for bringing the projects and techniques to life.

Thanks also to Lynne Rowe, Claire Crompton, Michelle Pickering, Lindsay Kaubi and Ann Barrett for their editorial work and index.